ADVANCE
BELIEF AND *CONFIDENCE*

"In *Belief and Confidence,* Ron Schiller makes a number of significant contributions to the body of knowledge in the fundraising profession. Among those contributions is his elucidation of the role of fundraiser as facilitator rather than solicitor and the act of fundraising as forging a partnership rather than transacting a gift. Perhaps most important, Schiller offers the master key to unlocking the philanthropic partnership by sharing profound insights from donors themselves about their motivations and expectations, their decision making and prioritization, their satisfaction and even frustration in choosing to make a significant gift to a given organization."

—**John Lippincott,** President Emeritus, Council for Advancement and Support of Education (CASE)

———————————————

"*Belief and Confidence* is the perfect title for this excellent guidebook for the philanthropist and nonprofit executive. It captures the essential ingredients for creating a successful philanthropic partnership. An excellent read!"

—**Ann Ziff,** Philanthropist

———————————————

"Significant philanthropy has intellectual, values-driven, and emotional components, for philanthropists and for those encouraging philanthropy alike. Ron Schiller builds on these components to illuminate the meaning of philanthropy and how to make the most gratifying and meaningful gifts a reality."

—**Robert J. Zimmer,** President, University of Chicago

ADVANCE PRAISE FOR
BELIEF AND *CONFIDENCE*

"In his new book on how and why major donors give, Ron Schiller shares invaluable lessons for philanthropists and nonprofits throughout the world. It is a must-read for understanding how to create satisfying and lasting partnerships that strengthen philanthropy and grow generosity."

—**Carol Adelman,** Director, Center for Global Prosperity, Hudson Institute

———————————

"The scriptures tell us 'it is more blessed to give than to receive.' Ron Schiller, in this remarkable anecdote-filled primer on philanthropy, takes that famed saying a couple of important and worthy steps further. Not only does he outline the values and satisfaction of philanthropy, but he also describes the techniques and best practices of the recipient. He argues that both parties must forge a partnership—creating mutual confidence and a stake in one another's beliefs. A must-read for nonprofit development officials and committees as well as donors hoping to benefit the public welfare."

—**Ann M. Korologos,** Nonprofit Leader and Former U.S. Secretary of Labor

———————————

"Ron Schiller's new book does something very important. It explores the ways in which significant gifts are made, from the perspectives of both the recipient and the philanthropist, and it demonstrates that these perspectives must ultimately be one and the same and rooted in trust. Donors do not make gifts, especially large gifts, because some fundraiser very cleverly talked them into it. Any fundraiser who thinks and acts otherwise is doomed to failure. Instead, both the organizational representatives and the philanthropist need to know themselves and one another in terms that Schiller describes as *belief* and *confidence*. To prove the case, he introduces readers to some wonderful and generous people who describe their experiences."

—**Don Randel,** President Emeritus, Andrew W. Mellon Foundation

BELIEF AND CONFIDENCE

BELIEF AND CONFIDENCE

Donors Talk About Successful Philanthropic Partnership

By Ronald J. Schiller

WASHINGTON, D.C.

Limit of Liability/Disclaimer: While the publisher and author have used their best efforts in
preparing this book, they make no representations or warranties in respect to the accuracy or
completeness of the contents of this book. Neither the publisher nor the author is engaged
in rendering legal, accounting or other professional legal or financial services. If legal advice
or other expert assistance is required, the services of a competent professional should be
sought.

Book design: O2 LAB · *o2lab.com*
Cover illustration: Caio Fonseca
Art Director: Angela Carpenter Gildner
Editorial Director: Doug Goldenberg-Hart

COUNCIL FOR ADVANCEMENT
AND SUPPORT OF EDUCATION®

CASE
1307 New York Avenue, NW
Suite 1000
Washington, DC 20005–4701

CASE Europe
3rd Floor, Paxton House
30 Artillery Lane
London E1 7LS
United Kingdom

www.case.org

CASE Asia-Pacific
Unit 05–03
Shaw Foundation
Alumni House
11 Kent Ridge Drive
Singapore 119244

CASE América Latina
Berlín 18 4to piso, Colonia Juárez
Código Postal 06600, México D.F.
Delegación Cuauhtémoc
México

CONTENTS

Section III: Facilitators: Staff and Volunteers— Development and Beyond

Section IV: Philanthropist to Philanthropist

Section V: Facilitators: What Can I Do?

PREFACE

Belief and Confidence: Donors Talk About Successful Philanthropic Partnership is written for philanthropically minded individuals and families and for all current and emerging nonprofit leaders who want to experience the joy and satisfaction of engaging with philanthropists and supporting their work. While informed by my own experience and the experience of nonprofit professional colleagues, this book's lessons come primarily from philanthropists.

Highly active board members and donors share with us details of their most satisfying transformational and major gift experiences and highlight the factors that distinguish these experiences, and the motivations behind them, from the rest. For the purposes of this book, transformational gifts are those, regardless of absolute dollar value, that are among the largest gifts a particular organization has *received* and that allow that organization to expand capacity to fulfill mission in an extraordinary way (beyond that which would be possible through gifts in the range regularly received by the organization). Major gifts, for the purposes of this book, are the largest gifts ever *made* by those interviewed.

BACKGROUND

Many articles and books have been written by fundraisers about how to cultivate and solicit major and transformational gifts. These, together with conferences and other training programs, contribute to a nonprofit professional's or fundraising volunteer's understanding of how to work with donors and potential donors. Much less is written on the subject of philanthropic partnership—less still that draws primarily on the perspectives and direct input of leading philanthropists. My entire career in fundraising, informed at an early stage by the celebrated work in principal gift fundraising of Cornell University president Frank Rhodes and renowned fundraising expert Dave Dunlop, and along the way by Jerold Panas's book *Mega Gifts* (Emerson & Church, 2005) and by many other wonderful teachers and mentors, *especially philanthropists,* has instilled and reinforced a certainty that there is no room for an attitude of "us and them" when it comes to creating and supporting partnerships between organizations and their donors. For the most part, nonprofit organizations wouldn't exist without philanthropy, and they will not continue to thrive without generous individuals and families who give their time, talent, expertise, and financial resources. Philanthropists are at least as important to the future of nonprofit organizations as any fundraiser or other organizational leader. Philanthropists and organizational leaders accomplish something together that neither could without the other.

Understanding of how to cultivate and solicit transformational and major gifts from individuals and families has improved as development has become more professionalized. The growth of the profession has included expansion of educational opportunities, allowing for improved communication of successful practices. It has also included great strides in donor stewardship—the critically important work that follows successful solicitation of a gift and goes well beyond gratitude and recognition. When we take the time to show donors that their gifts have been used wisely and well—when we share the results and impact of their investments—they are much more inclined to give again, and to give more.

During my career as a chief development officer and in my work as a board member, I have established several principal gift programs—programs focused on an institution's highest-level donors. Some of these programs focused on gifts of $5,000 and above; others focused on gifts of $5 million and above. In this work, and especially since moving to Aspen, Colorado, I have had the privilege of interacting with dozens of the wealthiest and most generous philanthropists in our nation and world.

Most nonprofit professionals who have played a lead role in securing a large gift can describe how the gift was cultivated and solicited, how the gift was recognized, and how the gift was stewarded. They can also talk about how the donor responded at various moments in the process, and what the donor has said, at least to them, about the gift since the gift was made.

Most donors who have made multiple gifts to multiple organizations can readily describe why they made these gifts. They can also usually describe whether and how they were thanked, whether they would make another gift, and why or why not.

But nonprofit professionals and volunteers rarely ask, and donors rarely discuss, how a giving experience compared to other giving experiences, including those at other organizations, and how they come to decisions about the few organizations with which they form their deepest philanthropic partnerships. Incorporating the words of "serial" philanthropists—donors who have made large gifts multiple times and to a variety of organizations—this book describes the factors that set donors' most satisfying and, in their view, successful transformational and major giving experiences apart.

RESEARCH/METHODOLOGY

This book draws on 30 years of work in the field of philanthropy. Philanthropists who informed and contributed to this book are donors across the United States and abroad. Their philanthropy also spans every part of the nonprofit sector, from arts and culture, to health care, to education, to global causes such as conservation, to social and community services. They have collectively made hundreds of gifts in the four-, five-, six-, and seven-figure ranges; almost 100 gifts in the eight-figure range; several in the nine-figure range; and one in the 10-figure range.

Those interviewed for the book answered the following questions:

- How many organizations do you support on a regular basis?
- How many have you supported at least once in the past 10 years?
- On how many boards do you currently sit?
- On how many have you sat in the past 10 years?
- How many organizations have received from you what you consider a transformational gift, over the past 10 years?
- Of these organizations, in how many have you or your spouse/partner been involved as a board member?
- What are the largest gifts you've ever made?
- Were they to organizations where you're involved as a volunteer?
- What are the main contributors to the belief and confidence you need and want in deciding to make a large and/or transformational gift?
- What are the main detractors from belief and confidence that would prevent you from making a large and/or transformational gift?

- Of all the philanthropic giving experiences of your lifetime, which one or ones would you describe as the most satisfying/rewarding?
- Why? What set them apart from the others?
- What, by contrast, is/are the *least satisfying* giving experience(s) you've ever had?
- What two or three things would you say to philanthropists who are just starting down the path of major giving, in terms of the most important and/or surprising lessons you've learned about what makes a giving experience satisfying and, in your view, successful?

Each interview was structured as a discussion into which I wove the questions above. My objective was to elicit anecdotes and stories that illustrated answers, and to allow those stories to lead us into deep conversation about the values and motivations driving giving choices, and how these had been shaped over time by experiences both positive and negative.

HOW THE BOOK IS ORGANIZED

The book is in five sections. The first three describe areas of belief and confidence, and the last two describe how to create environments with high levels of belief and confidence in which philanthropic partnership thrives.

The first three sections comprise 16 chapters, each presenting an aspect of belief or confidence, a description of what happens when this belief or confidence is missing, and an illustration of what is possible when it is strong.

The fourth section of the book, in three chapters, contains words of wisdom that leading philanthropists offered to those starting down the path of major giving.

The fifth section of the book, in 12 chapters, talks about what those engaged in nonprofit organizations as volunteers, administrators, and staff members—those taking on the responsibility for facilitating or enabling philanthropy—can do to contribute to stronger belief and confidence and to create environments in which philanthropic partnership thrives.

Belief and Confidence is a guide to all those engaged in philanthropy, as donors, nonprofit leaders, fundraising professionals, board members, and other volunteers. It illustrates the value in shifting focus away from chasing wealth and in the direction of enabling philanthropy. It encourages all involved in philanthropy to expand their thinking about cultivation and solicitation and to focus on building strong and lasting philanthropic partnerships, rooted in environments filled with belief and confidence. Embracing a role of facilitating partnership, those charged with raising funds will move beyond a focus on gifts that meet short-term organizational objectives to relationships that meet short-term goals while allowing donors to make the fullest expression of their philanthropic nature and intentions. When such partnerships flourish, donors provide leadership in giving—joyfully, with great satisfaction, and in many cases, *without even being asked.*

My hope, and the hope of all those interviewed, is that nonprofit leaders and philanthropists alike will find insights that lead to greater belief and confidence, more fulfilling philanthropic partnerships, and, as a result, increased philanthropic support of the organizations, leaders, and ideas that can drive the greatest improvements in the human condition.

ACKNOWLEDGMENTS

My first mentor in fundraising, Dave Dunlop, taught me about philanthropic partnership through his words, but especially through his actions. Everything he did and said made clear that the role of development professional and development volunteer, in major and transformational gift fundraising, is the role of enabler, facilitator, liaison. It rarely emphasizes solicitation, and it is never the role of arm-twister.

Tom Sokol, professor emeritus at Cornell University, another valued mentor and friend, asked me in the mid-1980s to take on the project of raising funds for a Cornell University Glee Club concert tour of Asia. Though most gifts were in the $50 to $100 range, hundreds of donors came together to make something happen that no one had previously thought possible. They transformed the fundraising capacity and ambition of the Glee Club, and in doing so they transformed the lives of the 100 students and alumni who went on that tour. One graduate from the Class of 1921 not only supported us, but also accompanied us on the tour, at the age of 90. I'll never forget the pride and joy on his face as he joined us on the stage. Many of the lessons in this book, from leading philanthropists across the country, hold true for fundraising at all levels. They show that giving can be at least as satisfying for the donor as for the organization that receives the gift.

These two men, among many other colleagues and friends, introduced me to the joy of philanthropic partnership—the magic of what can happen when nonprofit organization and donor come together to accomplish something that neither could do without the other. That joy has been reinforced every week for 30 years, as philanthropist after philanthropist has shown me the importance—to them, and not just to recipient organizations—of successful philanthropic partnership. Most of my closest friends are philanthropists, whether giving hundreds of dollars or tens of millions of dollars annually. Philanthropists—those who love humanity and express that by supporting society through partnership with nonprofit organizations—are the principal source of the abundance of joy I have experienced and continue to experience in my work.

I am grateful to all of them for the lessons they have taught me that inform this book. I am especially grateful to the leading philanthropists across the country who made generous contributions of time, thought, and encouragement as I worked on this project; many of them are quoted.

I'm indebted to readers Tim Child, Alan Fletcher, and Michael Vann, who gave intelligent, critical feedback, and to Robert Hurst for his contributions to Chapter 26.

The painting on the cover is by Caio Fonseca, whose friendship I treasure, and whose art is a constant inspiration.

I am grateful to CASE's Doug Goldenberg-Hart for his enthusiastic support throughout the project and to Amy Marks for her careful reading and excellent suggestions.

My parents taught me, through words and by example, to be a giving person. They always gave and continue to give when they see a need, without worrying about whether they can "afford" the gift. And it always seems to work out, as the rewards of giving far exceed the cost. They also taught me a lesson fundamental to philanthropic partnership: The appropriate response to each and every gift, no matter how large or small, is "Thank you."

Unwavering support for this book came, as it comes each day in every aspect of my life, from my husband, Alan Fletcher.

One of my most treasured memories is of philanthropists and friends Matthew and Kay Bucksbaum sitting in Aspen's historic Hotel Jerome, announcing their transformational gift of $25 million to the Aspen Music Festival and School. With tears making his kind and generous eyes sparkle, and with one tear gently rolling down his cheek, Matt praised the students, faculty, board, and president of the AMFS for their roles in making the gift happen. "We're just so grateful that we're able to do this," he said, with a smile even bigger than the one that seemed always to greet everyone who met him. This book is dedicated to him, with thanks for all he taught us about philanthropic partnership. Thank you, Matt.

INTRODUCTION

At the beginning of my career in fundraising, Dave Dunlop planted the seed of this book. "Givers make their largest gifts in support of ideas in which they believe and have confidence, and which are being pursued by people in whom they believe and have confidence," he said. For over three decades, this sentence has guided my approach to work with nonprofit organizations and with leading philanthropists. I've come to see that environments in which major and transformational giving thrive are marked by high levels of belief and confidence *across multiple dimensions* and on the part of their donors, leaders, staff, *and* volunteers. This book discusses 16 of them.

Philanthropists and those who facilitate their giving are believers. They believe in the power and importance of giving, they believe in the missions of the organizations they serve, and they share the visions of the leaders with whom they partner. Belief is powerful; it allows donors and leaders to dream great dreams about transforming organizations and improving quality of life. But vision without strategy is wishful thinking. Belief without confidence—confidence borne of due diligence and grounded in trust—can lead to unsuccessful and disappointing giving experiences.

As Harold J. "Si" Seymour (1966) wrote in his highly influential book, *Designs for Fund-Raising,* "Giving is prompted emotionally and then rationalized. The heart has to prompt the mind to go where logic points the way" (p. 29). Belief provides the emotional spark, and confidence provides the rational structure.

Belief coupled with confidence paves the way to involvement, and involvement further strengthens both. Strong belief and confidence, combined with deep engagement, create the possibility of philanthropic partnership, described below and throughout the book. The largest gifts then spring naturally from a mutual desire—on the part of the organization and the philanthropist—to combine resources to get something done.

Creating an environment filled with belief and confidence is far from a simple proposition. Belief and confidence must be strong internally as well as externally, built in the context of a highly competitive environment, and nurtured and sustained by many individuals, even through leadership transitions.

Increasing belief and confidence in one area will usually lead to increases in other areas, creating an upward spiral. Building a culture filled with belief and confidence where that culture does not exist is difficult. Once built, however, the success it generates breeds greater success and continuously reinforces the culture. Leaders willing to sacrifice long-term potential for short-term gain will threaten the culture, but philanthropists, who usually take the long view, and facilitators of philanthropy who have lived in a healthy culture, will work hard to preserve a culture of philanthropic partnership once they have found it or built it.

TYPES OF BELIEF AND CONFIDENCE

The book opens with eight chapters describing *donor* belief and confidence:

- Belief in the importance of giving
- Confidence in personal financial circumstances—present and future
- Confidence in other personal circumstances
- Belief in mission
- Confidence in leaders
- Belief in vision and confidence in strategy
- Confidence in organizational financial planning and stability—present and future
- Confidence in the capacity to raise additional funds

The next five chapters describe belief and confidence required of *organizational leaders:*

- Belief that the organization is worthy of philanthropic investment
- Belief and confidence in each other's leadership, vision, strategy, and planning
- Confidence in the CDO and development program
- Confidence in capacity to meet fundraising goals
- Belief in philanthropic partnership

The final group of dimensions of belief and confidence are those required of *staff members and volunteers*—including those outside of the fundraising program:

- Belief in mission
- Confidence in leaders, plans and goals
- Belief that individual contributions make a difference

Belief and confidence in some, even many, dimensions may be insufficient to overcome lack of belief or confidence in even one.

PHILANTHROPIC PARTNERSHIP AND SELF-SOLICITATION

The most striking finding in my discussions with leading philanthropists, consistent with my experience of many years, but notable in its prevalence, is that almost every major and transformational gift described as highly satisfying and/or most successful was also described by the donors as *self-solicited*. Exploring this donor perspective further, with both donors and with organizational leaders most deeply involved in work with top donors, it became clear that environments marked by high levels of belief and confidence produce philanthropic partnership: a culture in which both organizational leaders and donors talk about each other as partners. There is no "us and them." Philanthropic partnership *blurs the line between solicitation and self-solicitation.* There is rarely a moment of asking because the depth of partnership often makes the "ask" irrelevant.

"Most of our gifts have been self-investigated and self-initiated," says philanthropist Dennis Keller, speaking of his family's giving, which has included nearly a dozen eight-figure gifts. "The best way, that has the happiest reverberations for philanthropists and organizations, is to encourage deep engagement through which philanthropists figure out what they want to do based on their core beliefs and informed desires to help."

"We've given large gifts in response to requests," adds philanthropist Mellody Hobson. "But most of our largest gifts have been self-initiated. Our time is precious, and we don't want unsolicited requests—for financial resources, and especially for time. Because of our focus, involvement, and firsthand experience with the work of the organizations we support at the highest levels, we know what is needed."

Jason Franklin, philanthropist and executive director of Bolder Giving, agrees. "Gifts can be both solicited and self-solicited at the same time. Engaged donors develop an intention to give before an 'ask' is even articulated. In many cases they will express this intention before anyone makes an 'ask.' And even when the subject is raised by a solicitor, in the donor's mind the gift has already been made."

OPPORTUNITY AND IMPACT

A valuable and often-heard saying in the world of philanthropy is that donors don't give major gifts to organizations that *have* needs, but rather to organizations that *meet* needs. Leading philanthropists go further to say that "need" is the wrong emphasis altogether; instead, "opportunity" is what motivates both sides in a philanthropic partnership. When philanthropists see and understand opportunity—whether they were the first to see it, an organizational leader was first, or they came to a full understanding of an opportunity together—they will often step up with financial support before anyone has the chance to make an "ask."

It is not uncommon for a philanthropist to begin with an idea, *even without an organizational partner in mind,* and then to find the best partner or partners to implement the idea. Especially in these cases, philanthropists' intentions are to give to society *through* the organization as much as to make a gift *to* the organization. We will see numerous examples of this in the pages ahead.

THAT SOUNDS GREAT, BUT WHAT CAN I DO?

Philanthropists, along with those who facilitate their giving—organizational leaders, staff members, and volunteers—all play important roles in building belief and confidence and in creating and sustaining a culture of philanthropic partnership.

Philanthropist to philanthropist

Philanthropists' advice to current and emerging philanthropists falls into three categories: find your passion, find your partner, and get involved.

When asked how to ensure the most satisfying and rewarding giving experiences, every philanthropist included the importance of shared *passion* for the mission. Most placed this above all other considerations. Find your passion—know what matters in your heart. Their satisfaction was ultimately derived from impact, but they consistently drew a straight line between potential for impact and passion. Without passion, interest in giving fades, and sustained philanthropic partnership is unlikely.

Finding the right *partner* was also consistently emphasized as crucial to success and satisfaction in philanthropy. There are a lot of great causes, but without the right organization, the right leaders, *and* the right vision and strategy, the full potential impact of any gift is diminished. Leaders must be competent, but there are plenty of intelligent, experienced and capable people leading nonprofit organizations. The ones who win the confidence and philanthropic support of leading donors are those who fully embrace them as partners. Philanthropists should not be looking for leaders who simply roll over and do what philanthropists tell them to do; leaders should not accept gifts that are not right for their organizations. Listening carefully to leaders who listen carefully to them, philanthropists find partners who inspire them and allow them to make their best possible contributions to society.

Among many insights, Jerold Panas's *Mega Gifts* demonstrated that individuals and families making the largest gifts were deeply engaged with the organizations that received those "mega" gifts (Panas, 2005). The importance of *involvement* holds true today. With the explosive growth in the number of nonprofit organizations, that involvement is more important than ever.

Involvement need not be in the form of board membership, though *more than 75 percent of the top gifts given by philanthropists interviewed went to organizations where they or a close family member sit or have sat on the board.* For some philanthropists, this was 100 percent—they don't make major or transformational gifts *unless* they also sit on the board. Involvement could be a close relationship with a president or other leader, or intimate knowledge of a program developed through years of benefit or other close association.

The role of the facilitator

Leaders—both administrative and board leaders—bear the greatest responsibility for building and maintaining an organization's culture, including its culture of philanthropy. Every single person associated with a nonprofit organization has some capacity to add to belief and confidence, as well as some capacity to reduce belief and confidence.

Those most directly involved in fundraising, when aiming for major and transformational gifts, do well to think of themselves as facilitators rather than solicitors. Their first responsibility is to create an environment filled with belief and confidence in which philanthropic partnerships form and thrive.

In creating and maintaining philanthropic partnership, the facilitator's single biggest mistake is failing to engage a donor early and often. Usually for the sake of expediency, but sometimes due to carelessness or due to a desire to keep donors at arm's length, those in the best positions to facilitate philanthropic partnership instead move forward with their plans and proposals, waiting until the end of the process to engage potential donors. This type of fundraising can work; indeed, it produces fundraising revenue all the time. But it rarely produces transformational gifts, and it never, in my experience, produces the largest gifts that donors will make during their lifetimes.

When fundraisers—whether staff members or volunteers—ask about the ideas and objectives of philanthropists, they are much better able to identify shared passions and objectives as well as to educate donors and expand their thinking. Donor ideas and experience will also sometimes assist the organization in developing an improved plan or a more compelling case for support. "Most fundraisers don't think to ask prospective donors about their ideas, or about what they are trying to accomplish with their philanthropy," says philanthropist Ann Ziff. "They miss an opportunity to gain potentially valuable input and information. Taking the time to learn about donor objectives allows for true dialogue and a more robust conversation. When organization and donor vision can be brought into alignment, some truly exciting things happen."

Lessons emerging from my conversations with leading philanthropists as well as with successful facilitators of philanthropic partnership also include:

- Don't chase wealthy people first; find philanthropists.
- Pay attention to philanthropic priority, not just wealth and affinity.
- Ask donors how to ask them, thank them and recognize them.
- Get donors involved.
- With boards, focus on collective responsibility.
- Introduce donors to colleagues.
- Introduce donors to each other—let them spread belief and confidence.
- Practice philanthropic partnership yourself.
- Consider your approach.
- Everyone has a role to play.

SUMMARY

Philanthropists are generous people, not only in financial terms but also in their advocacy for organizations they support. Not surprisingly, those interviewed in connection with this book began by saying that they were generally satisfied with all of their giving experiences. By the end of the interview, most had talked about multiple negative and often hurtful experiences, experiences that had at times diminished their belief and confidence in individual leaders, whole organizations, and even philanthropy more broadly. Because of their generosity of spirit, they made gifts, including major gifts, to organizations and leaders they believed to be good partners. Their negative experiences principally revolved around the discovery that those who solicited or received the gifts were not truly interested in a mutually beneficial long-term relationship—a philanthropic partnership—but rather in a more arms-length financial transaction.

By contrast, the best experiences were tied to relationships that involved true philanthropic partnerships supported by high levels of belief and confidence. These gifts were largely made to organizations described by donors in the first person, rather than in third-person distancing language: they talked about what "we" had accomplished—they together with the organization—rather than what "they"—the organization—had accomplished. Once philanthropists and fundraisers experience true philanthropic partnership, they won't settle for anything less.

One underlying belief and one underlying confidence were evident in every discussion with every philanthropist who contributed to this book:

- They *believe* that nonprofit organizations enable philanthropists to have greater impact, and philanthropists enable nonprofit organizations to have greater impact. Fundraising is not about separating people from their wealth; it is about enabling those who have decided they have something extra—whether $5 or $500,000,000—to demonstrate love of humanity through partnership with nonprofit organizations.
- They are *confident* that true philanthropic partnership results in tremendous satisfaction and joy for everyone involved.

An environment filled with belief and confidence and marked by philanthropic partnership leads to unprecedented levels of ambition and achievement, and success builds on success. In the following pages, philanthropists join me in providing advice to current and emerging philanthropists about how to find and create such environments. Their reflections on both satisfying and unsatisfying giving experiences provide lessons to all volunteers, administrators, and staff members involved in nonprofit organizations, each of whom has an important role to play in creating and sustaining such an environment for their organization.

If your objective is to give or raise enough money so that your organization never needs to raise money again, you can stop reading right here. This book is not for you. If you desire greater satisfaction and joy in giving, or if you want to enable successful and satisfying major and transformational gift philanthropy, read on.

Section I
PHILANTHROPISTS

Chapter 1

DONOR BELIEF IN THE IMPORTANCE OF GIVING

It's a simple statement, yet it all begins here: We need individuals and families who believe in the importance of giving for philanthropy to thrive.

Some people learn philanthropy from their families; some learn from the example of friends and colleagues they respect. Many are influenced by religious teachings. Some feel obliged to give, some express gratitude through giving, and some give because they feel blessed with more than they need.

The giving philosophies of leading philanthropists have had tremendous impact on the thinking of donors. A recent example is the Giving Pledge, "an effort to invite the wealthiest individuals and families in America to commit to giving the majority of their wealth to philanthropy" (see *givingpledge.org*). In his book *The Billionaire Who Wasn't,* Conor O'Clery (2007, p. 99) describes the "profound effect" of Andrew Carnegie's writings on Chuck Feeney, one of the leading philanthropists of our time, especially Carnegie's famous essay, "Wealth," first published in the *North American Review* in 1889. Several donors interviewed for this book talked about the impact of Carnegie's essay on their thinking.

Regardless of why they give, "serial" philanthropists share one attribute: they *believe* in the importance of giving.

"Other than supporting family, philanthropy is the most significant, the most beautiful thing we can do with our resources," says philanthropist Robert

Hurst. "We are privileged to have what we have, and it is such a blessing, but it also carries an obligation, and we feel that profoundly. We take our work with nonprofit organizations very seriously." "That means getting involved, giving time as well as money," adds philanthropist Soledad Hurst. "Though at times the work is intense and even frustrating, it is mostly rewarding, and the involvement allows us to enjoy our giving so much more."

Individuals and families with "extra" financial resources—resources above and beyond an amount required for the standard of living they desire—make a wide variety of choices about disposition of their surplus funds. Only some of these people are philanthropically minded. Nonprofit organizations need to be able to identify those who believe in the importance of giving.

The amount or percentage of someone's surplus wealth reveals little about how much or even whether that person will give, whether directly to those in need or through nonprofit organizations. High net worth is by no means a predictor of a charitable nature, nor is lack of wealth a predictor of unwillingness or inability to give. The best ways to identify philanthropists with potential to become major and transformational gift donors are to

- pay attention to those who are giving—regardless of level;
- give priority, in allocating resources, to those with demonstrated belief in philanthropy;
- engage philanthropists in identifying other philanthropists; and
- get out of the office and talk to donors.

WHEN IT'S MISSING

People who don't believe in the importance of giving don't give, or give reluctantly. They may develop this belief over time, and they should not be ignored, but fundraising efforts are more profitably focused on those who have demonstrated a charitable nature.

Others are not actively philanthropic at their current stage of life, focusing instead on building wealth for later giving. In most cases, they will share this information, if asked.

A great deal of staff and volunteer effort is spent on uncovering wealth and on ranking constituents—whether alumni, audience members or grateful patients, for example—according to their net worth. Fundraising campaign ratings are routinely assigned to potential donors, using a percentage of visible wealth as the principal guideline. Wealth is likely also to contribute to decisions about governing or advisory board appointments.

Wealth is of course an important factor. An organization launching a major fundraising campaign will need leadership giving from the board, and they will need many other donors with the capacity to make large gifts. But many organizations make the mistake of filling board seats, or filling major gift officer portfolios, with people of great wealth, without adequately understanding the extent of their belief in the importance of giving.

A charitable person with $10 million in net worth and a 20-year record of giving may be a much better prospective donor for a $1 million lead gift than a person with $1 billion in net worth and no record of giving.

WHEN IT'S STRONG

"It's so much fun," says one donor. "The only reason to make more money is to have more to give away and to be challenged to figure out how to give it in a smart way, where you can do the most good." "When we got married," says philanthropist Jeanette Lerman-Neubauer, "we said we were registered at Tufts, Brandeis and the University of Chicago!" Gerald Ratner, who died in 2014 at the age of 100, and who practiced law until he was 99, gave millions of dollars to the University of Chicago. At one recognition event, well into his 90s, Gerry told me, with a twinkle in his eye, "I have to keep working so I have enough to keep giving."

"I was never interested in money," says philanthropist Leonard Polonsky. "I was interested in survival. Once I had earned enough to meet my needs and the needs of my family, my attention turned to giving. I have no interest in accumulated wealth; my idea of living is to get rid of it." Another donor expressed his wish to give every last penny to the organizations he loves in this way: "My greatest wish is that the last check I write is for a donation and that the check bounces."

People who believe in the importance of giving love to give—time, advice drawn from expertise, and financial resources. The more they give, the more they give. People who believe in the importance of giving may give well beyond the "1 percent of visible wealth each year for five years" guideline routinely used to predict giving in a campaign.

This belief reinforces the belief of others. Some philanthropists developed this belief at a young age, influenced by family or religion or both. But all have had that belief reinforced and expanded as a result of the example, and the company, of others who share their belief.

Many philanthropists invest time and effort instilling a belief in giving, along with values related to their belief, in future generations. "When my colleagues and I established our foundation, we drew upon the core values of the company we had built, the company that was the source of the assets we now distribute," says philanthropist Bruce Clinton. "Commitment to consistently high product quality is first on our list. Through involving them in the foundation's work, we pass along our values to our grandchildren. My granddaughter recently decided to shift her giving from one organization to another. When we asked her why, she explained that, in her evaluation, the first organization's leaders were not doing a good job at following through on what they had promised. 'I think we'll get a better return from this new organization,' she explained. My fellow trustees and I were floored—she was eight years old!"

People who believe in giving don't necessarily love every gift, but they can't imagine stopping. Those who give and have a positive experience with a particular organization or a particular leader are much more likely to continue giving once a giving relationship is established.

"A donor once told me the story of a president of a small cultural organization visiting along with his development director," says fundraising professional Tim Child. "The organization had given this donor and his family many wonderful experiences over many years. When the president finally summoned the courage to ask for a gift, the ask was relatively small. The donor excused himself, went to his office, and returned with a check for $1 million. The donor's face absolutely lit up when he told me the story, in part because he had a mischievous sense of humor, in part because he cherished the memory of the shocked president rendered speechless, and most of all because the act of giving for him and his wife was an utterly joyous experience."

Chapter 2

DONOR CONFIDENCE IN PERSONAL FINANCIAL CIRCUMSTANCES— PRESENT AND FUTURE

Most philanthropists give priority to the financial well-being of their loved ones. When that well-being is threatened, they may withdraw from philanthropy until their confidence in family financial security is again firmly in place.

Philanthropists recognize the importance of their gifts to the financial health and planning of recipient organizations. Accordingly, they do not want to make promises they cannot keep. Levels of confidence in personal financial circumstances directly affect their decisions about how much to give and the length of the pledge period they will consider.

Many factors can affect confidence in financial circumstances. These range from general environmental factors to circumstances specific to individual donors and their families.

WHEN IT'S MISSING

Downturns and volatility in the economy shake donor confidence. Regardless of wealth, drops in the stock market, in home values and in general economic outlook create concern, if not fear.

Confidence can also suffer as the result of financial losses affecting individual donors. These include downturns in a specific industry, failure of a business, drop in the value of investments and losses in real estate assets, among others.

In the recent recession, for example, many donors experienced a sharp drop in the value of investments. While some fundraisers might have thought to themselves, "He lost $50 million, but he still has $100 million," the philanthropist justifiably thought, "I lost $50 million; what if I lose another $50 million, or even another $100 million?" It is confidence in tomorrow that matters more than value of assets today. When the economic outlook improved, regardless of whether asset values were fully or only partially restored, philanthropists regained confidence.

A shift into retirement also diminishes confidence, at least temporarily, as donors adjust to new income patterns and parameters.

A major health issue will likely shake donor confidence. Even with excellent insurance, health issues can involve significant costs and at the same time result in loss of income. Many individuals with high net worth also believe that they need to set aside substantial sums to cover procedures that will increasingly be considered elective or otherwise will not be covered by insurance.

The death of a family member creates instability, including financial insecurity. Estates can take years to settle, and control of assets may change. Confidence on many levels, including on a financial level, may take time to rebuild.

When confidence in financial circumstances is shaken, donors delay or defer gift decisions, reduce amounts given and avoid long-term commitments. Furthermore, they may be embarrassed by financial setbacks and not share this information, leading organizational leaders to mistake their reduced giving as a sign of lack of commitment to the organization. Rarely do philanthropists stop giving altogether, but they may reduce the number of organizations they support. When they do, those organizations that have earned the highest levels of their belief and confidence are the most likely to remain on the list.

WHEN IT'S STRONG

Numerous factors contribute to increased confidence in financial circumstances. These in turn lead to more confident and faster responses to gift proposals, higher likelihood of donor-initiated gift discussions, and larger and longer-term commitments. Increased confidence also leads to accelerated gifts—pledges paid off more quickly than promised, or outright gifts that had been planned for estate distribution after death.

A stable economy creates a general atmosphere of elevated confidence, as donors are much better able to predict what they will have next month and next year. An economy perceived to be stable and improving leads to yet more confidence. The effect on individuals and individual families will vary, but a strong economy generally boosts income as well as the value of securities, real estate and other investments.

The sale of a company or the conversion or planned conversion of other non-liquid assets into liquid assets can also boost confidence, often creating a level of disposable wealth not previously enjoyed, and sometimes allowing for more tax-advantaged gifts, including gift structures that provide income streams to donors or to family members and friends the donors want to support.

Many donors pointed out that major and transformational giving did not enter their minds until they were in their 60s or even 70s. Though for some this was tied to a lack of time, earlier in life, to devote to philanthropy, for several it was because they had not achieved a sense of confidence in their financial capacity to make such gifts until they had sold a company, realized a significant increase in the value of certain assets, or finalized an inheritance. Their giving, however, in most cases, followed passions they had developed over years if not decades. In some cases, then, confidence in financial circumstances may be one of the later areas of belief and confidence to be developed.

Another important aspect of confidence in financial circumstances is confidence about the amount one can afford to give. Financial advisers may have or appear to have a vested interest in advising gifts that are too small, to preserve the value of investments under management, for example. Fundraisers may have or appear to have a vested interest in advising gifts that are too large, to boost fundraising numbers. Philanthropists are sometimes at a loss as to who might give the best advice on the right amount to give.

To gain this confidence, some donors turn to philanthropic advisers, such as Bolder Giving. "We are donors talking to donors, connecting peers who believe in giving boldly," says Jason Franklin, executive director of Bolder Giving, an organization that assists donors in "thinking big, figuring out how much to give, and becoming more effective, strategic and satisfied givers."

When confidence in financial circumstances is high, donors make "stretch" gifts, make decisions more quickly, and make longer-term pledges, convinced that they will not let down organizational partners.

Chapter 3

DONOR CONFIDENCE IN OTHER PERSONAL CIRCUMSTANCES

A variety of other personal circumstances can affect donor confidence and readiness to engage in a major gift discussion. In addition to financial circumstances, discussed in Chapter 2, the biggest factor for many donors is time. Many do not want to give, even when their financial resources are considerable, until they have time to devote along with their dollars.

Other factors that can add to or detract from confidence include family and marital issues, health, and a host of other contributors to general sense of stability and well-being.

As with most levels of belief and confidence, the best guides are the donors themselves. It is best to take them at their word when they say they don't have time to serve on a board. If they are on a board and can't attend meetings, successful leaders find other ways to keep them informed. One board member with whom I worked served on numerous corporate boards, whose meetings often conflicted with ours. He constantly felt guilty, until I told him I would visit him after board meetings to keep him informed and to find ways he could contribute, given his time constraints. Several years later, when he retired, he joined the executive committee, and then he became chair of the board.

Donors also want room to breathe when the timing doesn't seem right for a gift discussion. A response of "no" or "not now" to a request may have nothing to do with the donor's philanthropic nature or commitment to an organization or a project. When donors have relationships with a variety of individuals in an organization, and when trust is high as a result, chances are good that they will talk with someone about personal circumstances that they might not feel comfortable sharing with everyone.

Donors appreciate acknowledgment of the kernels of truth inside of fear. For example, donors will often be afraid that a deluge of requests will follow the announcement of their first large gift. Telling them that their fear is unfounded won't help, nor will telling them not to worry. Having other donors coach them on how to handle increased requests, including helping them learn how to say "no," gets them past a legitimate fear, even if that fear has become exaggerated.

WHEN IT'S MISSING

Donors will often have personal circumstances that diminish their capacity or confidence in moving forward with a gift discussion, sometimes creating minor concerns, and sometimes major. They will not always be comfortable discussing those circumstances with organizational representatives. Belief and confidence in other areas, especially leadership, increase the chances that donors will feel comfortable sharing such details; if they are not comfortable, they may well give a different reason or no reason at all for delaying a gift discussion or denying a request.

Such circumstances might include impending divorce, other family troubles, a major health scare or impending litigation.

Religion, as discussed in Chapter 1, often contributes to belief and confidence in giving. Organizational leaders' failure to understand all of the aspects of a religious motivation, however, can lead to awkwardness. A family's religious convictions might cause them, for example, to wish for anonymity in giving. Presenting such a family with a proposal that includes a building rendering with their names in foot-tall, brightly lit lettering would produce awkwardness, if not shock.

Donors contemplating a gift to a private school, college or university where their child is currently enrolled may well want to avoid publicity that might embarrass their child. Several donors spoke of gifts they made anonymously for this reason. In some cases, they asked for permanent anonymity; in many cases, they delayed recognition—in the form of a named building, for example—until their child graduated.

WHEN IT'S STRONG

It is difficult to predict individual circumstances that might come into play and whether donors will or will not be comfortable sharing their personal circumstances. Some circumstances will add to confidence, and some might diminish confidence. The stronger the relationship between organizational leaders and donors, and the more careful leaders are in listening and in paying attention to the many variables that might affect confidence, the more ready they will be to respond to positive circumstances and to address negative circumstances in ways that restore sufficient confidence for gift discussions to proceed.

In the following example, donor and organization were able to address a concern unanticipated by either party until the gift conversation was very far along. After months of discussions about a very large gift, a donor—seemingly suddenly—expressed hesitation about announcing the gift. Thanks to a close relationship between one family member and one senior officer of the organization, the family representative revealed that the family, never having made a gift of that size before, was concerned that doing so would expose their young children to risk, including the possibility of kidnapping.

The head of development reached out to other families who had made very large gifts and learned that several of them had confronted the same fear. They had worked with outside advisers, without the nonprofit organization ever being aware, to ensure their security and bring them to a level of comfort that their children would indeed be safe. The development leader was able to connect these families, and after some consultation, the new donors proceeded with their gift. Organizational leaders learned an incredibly important lesson and thankfully had built a level of trust that allowed them to discover the reason for hesitation and address it to the family's satisfaction.

Another family shared a story of hesitation caused by their religious beliefs. They wanted to help a favorite organization with a capital campaign. As a rule, however, they did not name buildings, primarily due to their desire, rooted in religious conviction, to avoid appearing boastful. Sensitive to their faith, a faith that was the bedrock of their philanthropic motivation, organizational leaders listened carefully to their concerns and worked with them on an alternative—naming the building for someone the organization wished to honor for reasons that had nothing to do with philanthropy, but rather for service.

When pairing gifts of time and effort with financial gifts is important to donors, confidence in giving will not be high until that time is available.

"In 2007, I sold my bank and woke up a different person," says philanthropist Adrienne Arsht. "My giving at major levels really started then. I had the money to give *and* the time to focus on where to give. I don't want to be on a board in name only, nor do I give without involvement. I'm giving away money I earned, and philanthropy for me is not about just distributing money. I'm hands on." Organizations that benefit from Adrienne's giving also benefit tremendously from her ideas and from her expertise.

Waiting to bring time and treasure together also, for many donors, produces much greater satisfaction. "Involvement along with giving leads to more fulfilling and more enjoyable philanthropy," says philanthropist Charles Wall. "That is why I waited until I retired to start making major gifts."

Chapter 4

DONOR BELIEF IN MISSION

Donors consistently and without exception report high levels of belief in the missions of the organizations that receive priority in their giving decisions. In the case of organizations that receive their largest gifts and gifts they describe as transformational, donors talk about mission as something *shared* by them and the organization. The organization's mission, or at least part of the organization's mission, is something they embrace deeply and very personally. Most go even further, saying that they are *passionate* about these shared missions.

Belief in mission may be based in personal passion for a mission, and it may also be based in connection to a mission through a donor's source of wealth. Examples of the former are love of the arts, a concern for the environment or a desire to cure cancer due to experience with cancer in one's family. Examples of the latter include a desire to support organizations serving a community in which a donor's business is based or a desire to give to an area connected with the source of the donor's wealth. For example, says philanthropist Emily Pulitzer, "Since my resources come largely from journalism, part of my philanthropy is focused on supporting quality journalism. This includes support of the Pulitzer Center on Crisis Reporting."

WHEN IT'S MISSING

In every organization I've served, and virtually every organization with whom I've consulted, Bill Gates and Oprah Winfrey are listed as top prospective donors. When asked why they are there, inevitably the answer is that some development committee member, at some meeting long forgotten, mentioned that their brother's wife's cousin worked with someone who used to work at Microsoft or who used to cook for Oprah.

Organizations need development staff members and volunteers to identify individuals and families with wealth, especially those who are philanthropic, and Bill and Oprah certainly meet the criteria. But prospective donors must believe in the mission of the organization seeking to engage them. If a wealthy person appears on a prospective donor list, one should ask, "Does that person have any reason to care about this organization?" If not, the prospective donor should move to the bottom of the list, if not off the list altogether.

The most common mistake reported by philanthropists related to giving without passion for the mission involved giving in response to a friend, before thinking through whether the gift would have personal meaning. Such gifts are common among leading philanthropists at lower levels, including buying tables at galas, for example. But philanthropists urge emerging philanthropists to become more purposeful once moving into higher-level giving. "One of the most important lessons I learned along the way is to be proactive, rather than reactive to people asking," says one philanthropist.

Lack of mission alignment is also a major factor in turnover among development officers. Early in the evolution of the development profession, most people fell into development jobs, as training programs were few and far between. They fell into these positions, in most cases, at organizations where they had prior involvement, often as a donor or volunteer. As the profession has grown, more and more positions are filled with people seeking professional advancement, including title, responsibility and compensation. Title and compensation go only so far, however, and when mission alignment is not also strong, development officers struggle to maintain the drive required for success.

WHEN IT'S STRONG

As discussed in great detail in Chapter 17, philanthropists advise up-and-coming philanthropists to align giving with passion, giving to and through organizations whose missions allow full expression of that passion. Asked about the lessons they learned in their own philanthropic work that they most want to pass along, every philanthropist interviewed included "find and follow your passion," and most put this at the top of the list.

In short, this belief is essential to philanthropic partnership and to major and transformational giving.

Chapter 5

DONOR CONFIDENCE IN LEADERS

Major philanthropists consistently report strong relationships and high levels of confidence in leaders of the organizations that receive substantial shares of their philanthropy. These leaders vary—sometimes they are board members, sometimes CEOs, and sometimes leaders of the individual programs donors support. In most cases, they have confidence in all of the above.

"Know the individual or individuals you'll be dealing with," advises philanthropist Georgette Bennett. "Some are skilled leaders, and some are not. The wrong person won't excite your imagination and sustain your interest. In looking for partners to help us realize our philanthropic objectives, we evaluate not only the organization and its mission, but also the leaders with whom we'll be working. In some cases, we have followed those leaders to other organizations."

Leaders who themselves give substantial sums, such as board members, raise the confidence of potential donors simply through their example. A donor who has a trusting relationship with a board member is comforted by the fact that the board member has decided to make the organization a philanthropic priority.

The president and CEO of an organization is also a key contributor to donor confidence. Most philanthropists have strong relationships with the current CEOs of the organizations they support. "No matter who you are, it is flattering and reassuring when the president takes time to meet with you in person," say philanthropists Peter and Nancy Meinig. In the words of another leading philanthropist, "I want to look the CEO in the eye and know that she is going to make sure my gift is used in the way I intend."

"Almost all nonprofit organizations are run by well-meaning people," says philanthropist Jessica Fullerton. "But I like to see that extra something that shows they can accomplish what they want to do: high energy, vision, and great courage." "We back those who give 120 percent all of the time," adds philanthropist John Fullerton. "We are drawn to high-caliber leaders whose work is clearly a major part of their identity, particularly those capable of attracting and building a team of like-minded people."

Other philanthropists are more interested in the leaders who are directly involved in the day-to-day work of an organization. They want to know that the board and CEO are supportive, but most important to them is confidence in the people on the front line—whether the conductor of the orchestra, the head of the research laboratory, or the dean responsible for implementing a new program and recruiting the best and brightest faculty members. Besides giving donors a closer look at the impact of a gift, these relationships allow donors to share the emotional satisfaction of a gift's outcome with the people who helped shape and implement the project or program the gift was used to support.

Donors increasingly want to know that their gifts have measurable impact. They hold leaders accountable for the use of gifts. Also, they want to be proud of their affiliation with the organizations they support. Since leaders are the public and visible face of an organization, they want to be confident that leaders will add to that pride of affiliation.

WHEN IT'S MISSING

"Our family will not initiate a gift if we reach the conclusion that an organization isn't ready," says Dennis Keller. "We would reach such a conclusion if, in our evaluation, the project isn't right, the timing isn't right, the project isn't appropriately ambitious, or the organization is simply not prepared to execute successfully. Above all, if leadership isn't right, none of the rest matters. We're looking for a pole vault, and leadership is the first thing you look at in evaluating readiness for the jump."

Donors, including board members, occasionally overstep their authority. In some cases, this is due to lack of understanding of the proper division of responsibilities between board members and paid administrators. In others, it is because of lack of confidence in those managing the organization, including the implementation of gifts given by the donor. "It's your team that's going to make your gift work, not only you," adds philanthropist Bill Budinger. "If you feel you have to get into the weeds, you've got the wrong team."

Leadership vacuums can create a sense of instability, if not actual instability. In these cases, confidence may be diminished, if only temporarily.

WHEN IT'S STRONG

Philanthropist Joan Kroc made a gift through her estate of more than $200 million to National Public Radio. When I discussed this gift with her adviser, after her death, he told me that in all her giving, three simple elements came into play: the organization and its reputation, its vision for the future, and most important, the person who ran the organization. According to him, and reinforced by others who worked on that gift, she put her big "chips" on people she most admired, could relate to, and trust.

"The quality of leaders throughout an organization is a good indication of the quality of the CEO," says Charles Wall. "Nines hire tens, whereas fives hire fours. Excellent CEOs are not afraid of having strong people in the organization. They look for independent thinkers and people whose strengths will make them better and more successful as CEOs. Smart philanthropic investors look for quality throughout an organization."

When philanthropist David Booth made his $300 million gift to the University of Chicago, he emphasized the important role of faculty members in his success in business, in particular Eugene Fama. David's finance courses with Professor Fama and work as his research assistant were instrumental in some of David's early decisions about business, and Professor Fama stayed connected, sitting on David's company's board of directors. "The university has been a partner all along, so this is a partnership distribution," said David, in announcing his gift. "Personally, it's an incredibly great day for me," Professor Fama responded. "A person I admire and a friend of mine for 40 years is putting his name on an institution that's nourished me for 50 years" (Sider, 2008).

"One thing that all our most satisfying giving experiences have in common is product quality and consistency," says Bruce Clinton. "And that doesn't happen without quality leadership. The Chicago Symphony Orchestra speaks for itself. The Fairchild Tropical Botanic Garden is among the best in the world. Mayo Clinic is at the top of its game. A small, neighborhood organization with performance that is consistently off the charts will also inspire our support.

We've had relationships with leaders at all levels in many organizations. Those that sustain our interest and involvement are those who consistently perform at the highest levels."

Leadership transitions can create fundraising opportunities, as some donors accelerate gifts to honor an outgoing leader, and others become inspired and excited by a new leader. Board members involved in a presidential search have an opportunity to develop early confidence in a new leader and to instill that confidence in others.

Confidence in leaders also means trusting leaders to use gifts well, and letting them do their jobs. "Thankfully there aren't many, but we've all seen donors who dangle money and want to manage everything," adds Peter Meinig. "Donors should begin by making sure the right people are leading the organizations they support. Once they have that confidence, they need to trust those leaders. Presidents, backed up by their boards, should refuse gifts that come with too much donor control and interference. In one case, one of the organizations we support chose to return a large gift, and it was the right thing to do."

Chapter 6

DONOR BELIEF
IN VISION AND
CONFIDENCE IN STRATEGY

Philanthropic partnership is all about philanthropists and organizations accomplishing something together that they couldn't accomplish on their own. In addition to believing in mission and having confidence in leaders, those making major gifts report that they are inspired by vision that they share and that is backed up with detailed, careful and strategic planning.

Mission is not enough. An organization must regularly evaluate and update thinking on how best to fulfill its mission in a competitive and changing landscape. And smart, experienced leaders are not enough, without a clear and compelling vision rooted in ambitious yet believable plans.

Regular communication between donors and organizational leaders is a minimum requirement for building and maintaining shared belief in vision and confidence in planning. Organizations deepen this belief and confidence through engagement of donors in vision development and in planning—the earlier, the better.

They further build confidence through measurement and proof of impact. Leaders engaged in major and transformational gift fundraising should *expect* to build fact-based measurement into gift agreements. "When we've made transformational gifts, organizations have needed to enter into an agreement that includes regular and rigorous reporting and periodic outside peer review," says philanthropist Sandra Rotman.

New leaders bring new vision, and their vision can inject new energy and drive new and exciting strategic planning. Philanthropists with extensive giving experience point out, however, that their long-term philanthropic partnerships—the ones that lead to multiple large and transformational gifts—are with organizations that also have a unifying and sustained over-arching vision. Leaders come and go, but these organizations are marked by a strategic coherence in values that inform this overarching vision and adhere from generation to generation.

WHEN IT'S MISSING

Organizational leaders—programmatic leaders, in particular—are often reluctant to engage potential donors in planning, fearing that these individuals will exert inappropriate influence. Excluding donors, however, all but removes the opportunity to create a feeling of personal investment in a successful outcome, and it also deprives an organization of some potentially strong contributions to planning that draw on the experiences and perspectives of donors often capable of bringing more than money to the table.

Philanthropists bring financial resources, philanthropic objectives, and ideas to the table, and in many cases they also bring expertise. Failure to recognize expertise depresses donor confidence in plans and is an indication of a weak institution. "Over the years, I've worked on many new building projects in a very specialized part of the nonprofit sector," says one leading philanthropist. "Nevertheless, my local organization, when engaged in an important new building project, wanted my financial support but was not at all interested in the expertise I had developed nationally and internationally. I made a gift early in the process, but mistakes were made that could have been avoided with wider input." Diminished confidence led the donor to a significant contraction in future giving.

"Incongruity among board members is generally the result of one of two things—vision without effective leadership, or leadership without vision," says philanthropist Raymond J. McGuire. "Even when a leader is willing to engage board members and other donors in strategic planning, the lack of a clear, compelling and shared vision can create a challenging board dynamic and compromise the strategic planning process."

WHEN IT'S STRONG

"In our philanthropy, we look for innovation that can be tested, replicated, and scaled and, through scaling, become self-sustaining," says Jeanette Lerman-Neubauer. "We prefer partners whose strategic vision is aligned with our philanthropic objectives, whose leaders are committed to data analysis that measures progress against a specific plan and that enables them to fine-tune, replicate and scale."

"For example," Jeanette continues, "the Metropolitan Opera's Peter Gelb proposed an innovative idea: to transmit performances in high definition to movie theatres around the world. Though there were vocal skeptics, we saw a convincing business plan with unusual potential. It took five years for any of us to understand the full impact of what had been achieved. The ticket price point enabled both older and younger opera lovers to attend performances with more frequency, creating a more robust global opera community. Broadcasts entice out-of-towners to book opera house tickets and back-stage tours when they visit New York City. Young singers are exposed to casting directors, worldwide, resulting in accelerated career development. After nine years, the series now reaches more than 2,095 venues in 70 countries. There are approximately 250,000 to 300,000 simultaneous viewers per transmission. The Met has developed a nationwide program for students to attend *Live in HD* transmissions and study the music in their schools. The Met *Live in HD* is not only self-sustaining; it provides a significant new revenue stream."

When philanthropist David Tepper announced his gift of $55 million to Carnegie Mellon University in 2004, he said, "To come from Peabody High School and be able to do this in my life is just amazing. … Dean Dunn is making some fantastic and strategic changes to the school's curriculum and focus. He needs resources, and I wanted to be a part of it" ("A kid from Peabody High School," 2004). The donor did not consider his gift a transfer of money from his family to an organization but, rather, a partnership investment in the future of a school that now bears his name.

When Carnegie Mellon's Ken Dunn began his conversation with donor David Tepper, he hoped that David would become excited enough about his and the school's vision to make a major gift. He had no idea David would go on to make the largest gift, at the time, in the university's history. Rather than asking for a gift, Ken described his vision and then paused. In David's response, Ken understood that he had found a partner, and that David's principal concern would be making sure the vision could be realized.

"At the age of 16, I participated in The Experiment in International Living, now a part of World Learning," says philanthropist Ann Friedman. "That experience was among the most formative of my life. Several years ago, the organization found me, and they asked for a gift. I responded by saying that I'd really like to serve on the board. After serving on the board, I joined a task force aimed at building on The Experiment's 80-year record of accomplishment and rejuvenating its brand. Our research was extensive, and my involvement resulted in deep confidence in the outcomes. That confidence led my husband Tom and me to volunteer, without being asked, to support half the cost of the program for three years, with the provision that others match the funds. The response was tremendous, and the organization was able to raise the matching funds quickly. This gift is among the most transformational we've ever made."

Board members and other top donors who are deeply engaged in vision development and long-term planning often make the first gifts in support of major initiatives that result from such plans, and, as mentioned earlier in this book, *these gifts are often self-solicited*—that is, the engaged donor doesn't even wait to be asked.

Chapter 7

DONOR CONFIDENCE IN ORGANIZATIONAL FINANCIAL PLANNING AND STABILITY— PRESENT AND FUTURE

Philanthropists view major gifts as investments, where the return is measured by impact on society rather than growth in the donor's financial assets. But they are investments nonetheless, and the performance of these investments depends on financial strength and stability of the recipient organizations.

Major gifts, to be sure, enhance that financial position. But without a degree of stability outside of that provided by the gifts themselves, and unless the philanthropists in question are very close to the recipient organizations and intend their gifts as bailouts, donors will look for assurances that their investments will be well managed and can be used for the purposes intended. Confidence drops when they perceive a risk that their gifts will need to be redirected in order to address financial weakness or mismanagement.

WHEN IT'S MISSING

One donor told the story of an organization with a great project, but with no financial plan to sustain it. She was asked to fund the project for three years, but she was concerned by a lack of careful planning and by what seemed to her to be an unwise allocation of resources, given the organization's other needs. Her excitement about the idea, however, led her to offer one year, provided the organization was prepared to sustain the project into the future. She was told they were, only to learn later that their plan, at the time she made the one-year gift, was to come back to her after all, hoping she would love the project so much that she would solve their problem and continue annual funding. "If the allocation of resources isn't something you'd choose, and if you aren't persuaded otherwise by organizational leaders, then you're setting yourself up for heartache. The knot in my stomach was initially overcome by the belief in the idea of the project, but my initial instinct proved true. As exciting as the project was on some levels, it wasn't, after all, a smart allocation of resources on the part of the organization. My role at best would have been to continue to reward poor planning."

"We gave to one organization we loved," says one leading philanthropist, "but they were always in trouble. It became exhausting to bail out an organization that couldn't manage itself." "You need to be confident your money will be used wisely," adds Sandra Rotman. "When we weren't sure an organization was going to take good care of what we were going to give them, negotiations stopped."

"We take time to understand the financial plans and financial management of organizations we support with major gifts," says Nancy Meinig. "We've never had a disastrous experience, but in one case, we found that an organization whose mission we loved was simply not facing reality and was not being managed well. We turned our attention to other organizations."

"We involve our grandchildren in giving," Nancy continues. "We encourage them to begin with mission, then learn about leadership and vision, then do as much research as possible into finances. Without sound financial planning and management, and without confidence in how gifts will be used, a lot of money can be wasted that otherwise could be put to very good use."

Unfortunately, examples abound of organizations, evidently beyond the ability to manage themselves out of bad situations, that resort to "panic" fundraising, and at their peril. My colleagues and I refer to this type of fundraising as "Name a Stateroom on the Titanic" fundraising. Donors will throw $50, or maybe even $5,000, at an organization verging on bankruptcy, but rarely will they invest millions. They worked hard for that money, and they don't want to see it disappear overnight. Or they inherited the money, and they don't want to risk carrying guilt about squandering a fortune made possible by the hard work of their ancestors.

WHEN IT'S STRONG

The importance of this type of confidence is underscored by the success of organizations known for raising large gifts. Organizations that raise large gifts go on to raise more large gifts, as donors observe others making large investments that boost their own confidence in the wisdom of such an investment. Rarely do major donors express an unwillingness to give to an organization "because they raise lots of other large gifts." If they are not convinced that their gift will have an impact, as outlined in other chapters, they may choose to give to an organization with more clearly stated need. But the fact of other large gifts itself is not an obstacle, and is rather a confidence builder. When others deem an organization worthy of large gifts, they make a choice that inspires and/or confirms the choice of others to do the same. In short, success in major gift fundraising breeds more success in major gift fundraising. Major gift donors join winning teams.

Chapter 8

DONOR CONFIDENCE IN ORGANIZATIONAL CAPACITY TO RAISE ADDITIONAL FUNDS

Donors willing to take a leap of faith and make lead gifts in the early stages of fundraising efforts are praiseworthy. If you know such donors, put down this book and write them a note, just to let them know how rare and wonderful they are!

Successful organizations plan carefully before soliciting lead gifts, ensuring that they have the capacity to follow through. This starts with agreement among leaders that a project for which lead gifts are sought is a priority. Then and only then do leaders develop financial plans that identify potential donors as well as alternative funding sources, should fundraising not go as planned. Once agreement is reached on the financial plan, and once leaders agree there is sufficient fundraising potential and backup funding available to ensure success, they talk with lead donors.

Plans do not always allow for backup funding. In this event, wise leaders avoid making promises to lead donors that they cannot keep; broken promises related to gifts are betrayals of confidence. They are willing to delay project commencement, or to delay pledge payment requirements, or to have an agreement in place on an alternate use of funds should the project not come to fruition. But above all, they are honest and fully transparent with lead donors. Donors are almost always ready to accept risk, but they won't appreciate negative surprises, and they are highly unlikely to be there the next time, regardless of how solid future plans might be.

In summary, this confidence is built over time, earned with each project and easily lost. Many major donors have had at least one negative experience. Philanthropists stick with organizations and leaders who resist the temptation to get today's gift but lose tomorrow's confidence.

WHEN IT'S MISSING

"When donors get the feeling that organizations are relying on them to take care of everything, it puts their relationship at risk," says one philanthropist. "I'm happy to help," he adds, "but coming back to me too many times without getting others involved is exhausting. I once made a $5 million gift, which I initiated, and it fully funded a project that I thought was important. Almost immediately, the organization was launching another project and needed to raise $15 million. They came back to me for a lead gift. I told them I would do something, but they should have involved some others first. It was a frustrating experience."

When organizations accept lead gifts without the capacity to raise the full amount required to complete a project and fulfill promises made to lead donors, they diminish donor confidence in the organization and in the whole development profession. They raise levels of skepticism, and they reduce the number of these faithful, critical believers.

WHEN IT'S STRONG

With this confidence, organizations get projects off the ground, build confidence among other potential donors, build momentum, and realize objectives previously considered out of reach.

"Lead gifts are critical to the success of ambitious projects," says philanthropist Andrew Alper. "Before making a lead gift, donors need confidence in an organization's capacity to raise the rest of the funds that will be required for the project, and this means that the organization's leaders must develop clear and believable plans for fundraising beyond the lead gift or gifts. When I've made lead gifts, I've done all I can to assure myself that the organization has the donor prospects, cultivation strategy and solicitation plans in place to achieve the overall philanthropic goal."

Philanthropist Mike Murray agrees. "A lead gift is a vote of confidence. At the same time, it requires a leap of faith. When we have made lead gifts, it has been because we love an organization and want its plans to succeed, but also because our faith has been bolstered by confidence in the management and the board and by belief that goals for the project are realistic."

Section II

FACILITATORS: ORGANIZATIONAL LEADERS

Chapter 9

BELIEF AMONG LEADERS THAT THE ORGANIZATION IS WORTHY OF PHILANTHROPIC INVESTMENT

Organizations that secure large gifts on a consistent basis generally share a common trait—leaders, usually including the CEO, the chief development officer, and the board chair, are bullish about big gifts. Not only are they willing to ask at the highest levels, but they believe deeply that their organizations are worthy of these gifts. They carry that belief into ambitious strategic planning, focused fundraising planning, and messaging. They think about and talk about these gifts well before the gifts are realized. They are not the least bit deterred by the lack of gifts at such levels in the organization's history.

This is true whether the scale of top gifts is $5,000 or $50 million. Transformational gifts rarely happen without leaders believing they will happen and backing up those beliefs with plans for such gifts.

"'Big gift' means different things to different people," says Jason Franklin. "For most fundraisers, success requires accepting that they will be asking for gifts beyond—often well beyond—a level they will ever be able to give themselves. They must raise their sights to the highest level possible for their organizations."

WHEN IT'S MISSING

Fundraisers may think their biggest challenge is in building donor belief and confidence, but often donors have greater belief and confidence than organizational leaders. "Donors are usually the easiest when it comes to sight-raising," says Curt Simic, a colleague who has worked with dozens of transformational gift donors and several leading fundraising programs, including Indiana University and the University of California, Berkeley. "Getting an organization's leadership to raise their sights must be accomplished first. *Otherwise, donors will sit on the sidelines or gravitate to other organizations with bold vision and leadership.*"

"Donors who have a history with the organization can be among the most helpful in raising the sights of internal leaders," he adds.

WHEN IT'S STRONG

One president I know accepted a position with an organization that was contemplating a major capital campaign. The largest gift in the organization's history was $4 million, but the president believed the organization, given its ambition and its potential, should test a $75 million campaign. He further understood that such a campaign would be unsuccessful without a lead gift of $25 million. The organization's previous campaign total was $12 million, so almost everyone other than the president thought $25 million wasn't even worth considering. Many attempted to discourage him from asking at such a level. Undeterred, the president built the case, engaged a family who themselves had never made or contemplated a gift on this scale, and succeeded in securing the commitment. In a press conference announcing the gift, the donor commented on the president's unflagging belief in the project, in the organization, and in the transformational impact the gift would have. "He was a tiger."

In another organization, a lead gift was secured in the nucleus phase of a campaign, and the gift was the largest gift the organization had ever received. Both the president and the campaign chair requested that the gift not be counted in the nucleus phase amount, concerned that the scale of the gift would cause the organization to set a campaign goal beyond reach. The chief development officer, rather than arguing, focused the development team's efforts on securing the next lead gift. That gift, also among the largest ever received by the organization, elicited a different response from the same president and campaign chair. Instead of asking that the gift be excluded, they asked, "Who do you think will make the third lead gift?" Their belief and confidence in the organization's worthiness of gifts at this level, and ability to secure such gifts, was changed forever. And the organization completed a record-breaking campaign.

Major philanthropists do not make gifts in order to fill empty boxes on the gift table! Upon asking for ideas that would drive a nine-figure gift, the chief development officer of one organization found that the majority of internal leaders believed such a gift to be so far out of the reach of the organization that planning would be a waste of time. When organizational leaders developed a transformational program requiring several hundred million dollars of investment, a donor responded with the organization's first nine-figure gift. The organization not only went on to secure another nine-figure gift, but its success in securing eight-figure investments soared, fueled by ambitious and inspirational strategic planning, fundraising planning focused on donors with this level of capacity, and leaders who asked with contagious belief and confidence.

Chapter 10

BELIEF AND CONFIDENCE AMONG LEADERS IN EACH OTHER'S LEADERSHIP, VISION, STRATEGY AND PLANNING

Philanthropic partners—the individuals, families and institutional donors who make major and transformational investments—develop multiple relationships with organizational leaders over time. Those who have given over years, or decades, will have relationships well beyond those known by the CEO or chief development officer. Trying to control the flow and content of communication between organizational leaders and these partners is futile. When organizational leaders get along well and complement each other, donors know. When organizational leaders disagree, even if not publicly, donors know.

Administrative and board leaders, working in harmony, have the capacity to build and reinforce extraordinary levels of belief and confidence. At the same time, any individual leader has the capacity to destroy, or significantly diminish, belief and confidence.

WHEN IT'S MISSING

Little can diminish belief and confidence across internal *and* external constituents more quickly and more harmfully than lack of confidence among organizational leaders. Disagreements between a board chair and the president that become public, votes of no confidence, lack of mutual respect among members of an executive team, division within boards, and competition among leaders of various programs that causes one leader to disparage another are examples of a breakdown in confidence that causes philanthropic partners to retreat and wait out the storm.

Lack of consensus around organizational priorities and lack of genuine support for strategic objectives, even outside a leader's area of responsibility, lead donors to question an organization's capacity to follow through on projects and to complete them in a cost-effective manner. Real or perceived silos, real or perceived unproductive competition, forces appearing to be working against an initiative in which a donor is interested, and indications that a respected leader finds another organizational leader weak or incompetent suggest to philanthropic partners a reasonable to high likelihood of ineffective deployment of financial resources and failed outcomes.

Beyond being dishonest, attempts to gloss over or hide lack of internal consensus and confidence rarely succeed and have the potential to destroy a philanthropic partnership irreversibly. The more relationships the donor has with organizational leaders, the more likely such attempts will fail.

Ideally, a degree of internal consensus is reached prior to engaging philanthropic partners. This need not be complete; indeed, allowing philanthropic partners to take part in deliberations can often increase their sense of ownership of outcomes. Regardless of whether donors are involved before or after consensus is reached, leaders must be willing to support—or at least not undermine—consensus decisions once they are made. For major organizational objectives, involving or at least informing a broad set of leaders increases the likelihood they will augment rather than detract from donor confidence when asked their opinion, even when asked to comment on objectives in which they have little personal involvement.

When one leader gets ahead of others, failing to build consensus around a specific initiative, donor confidence in vision, strategy and planning can suffer. Donors know that success in most initiatives requires broad organizational support. If one or more key leaders are unaware or, worse, unsupportive of a project, donor confidence in the project's viability can be shaken to the point that donors are reluctant to make a philanthropic investment.

One colleague shared the story of a board member who was so inspired by a dean's and president's preliminary plans for a new facility presented early in their campaign process that he pledged a large lead gift, and the dean and the president accepted. The feasibility for supporting the new facility had not yet been studied, however, nor were plans for the new facility well formed. In the end, the facility turned out not to be a high priority for most other leaders in the organization; hence, it was not regarded as a high priority for the organization as a whole. Recognizing this, other donors backed away, and the organization struggled for many years to raise the remaining funds needed.

WHEN IT'S STRONG

"Involved with an organization for many years, I was well aware of the needs of the area in which I was most involved, but also aware of the lack of support of that area on the part of key leaders in other parts of the organization," says one leading philanthropist. "I agreed to an eight-figure gift—transformational for that area of the organization—but only after the new president and CEO promised me and the leader of that area the organization's full support. She and I were both fully aware of the lack of past mutual support among leaders, and I had confidence in her. She followed through on her promise, with a very happy result. It is one of the most successful gifts I've made. But without that leader-to-leader commitment within the organization, I wouldn't have made the gift, because it wouldn't have worked."

Finance staff, investment staff, board members, and others involved in financial planning are in a position to cast unfunded plans as perilous to an organization or as opportunities requiring additional investment or revised financing strategies. All nonprofit organizations, regardless of size of budget and size of endowment, face financial challenges. When members of a team have confidence in each other, and when their organization's finances are fundamentally stable, even if not as strong as they might like, they avoid unproductive hand-wringing and present financial challenges in an appropriate light, sustaining confidence in their organization as worthy of additional philanthropic investment.

Confidence in vision, strategy and planning that is shared among leaders across an organization signals several important things to donors, all of which build their confidence in giving:

- Plans have been carefully considered and vetted; they are not the result of one person's pipe dream.
- Multiple and varied perspectives have informed the plan, producing a stronger result.
- Leaders across the organization will marshal resources and lend support within their powers to ensure the project's success.

Chapter 11

CONFIDENCE AMONG LEADERS IN THE CDO AND THE DEVELOPMENT PROGRAM

Confidence in the chief development officer (CDO) and the development program among administrative and board leaders is critical to successful establishment and sustenance of a healthy environment for fundraising. Most important, CEOs must have high confidence in their CDO partners. When that confidence is missing, confidence among other leaders in the CDO and in the rest of the development program suffers.

In Chapter 1 of my last book, *The Chief Development Officer: Beyond Fundraising* (Rowman & Littlefield, 2013), I addressed this critical area of confidence:

An excellent partnership with the CEO is vital to organizational fundraising success, and it is *essential* to CDO job security. CDOs recognize the paramount importance of this relationship, investing great care in establishing and maintaining absolute and mutual trust, respect, and confidence. A board chairman put it this way: "The CDO has to vibrate on the same frequency as the CEO. It helps if this is true of other senior officers, but it must be true of the CDO."

CEOs must have complete confidence in their CDO partners. Loss of this inevitably leads to CDO departures and is a leading cause of transition in the position of CDO: in the 200 CDO transitions observed by those interviewed, loss of CEO confidence played a role in more than 90% of departures. "The basic problem was a disconnect between our CEO and CDO, and that led to a yawning chasm of distrust," said a CDO's direct report, describing the events leading up to her CDO being asked to step down. "With the CDO always feeling second-guessed by the CEO, everything around and under the CDO started to fracture."

The successful CDO has the confidence of other senior leaders as well. When it is lacking, the situation may become fatal for CDOs, especially if CEOs are forced to devote precious time and energy to mediating or working around weak or damaged CDO relationships. One trustee described a situation in which the CEO had to ask a CDO to step down due to an irreparable relationship between the CDO and the board chair, even though "the relationship between the CEO and CDO was excellent." A CEO in higher education spoke of a former CDO who "wanted complete control of everything related to development." The CDO "made it clear in executive staff meetings, both verbally and through his body language, that he was not interested in the business of other units, and that other executive staff members should run their own units and leave him alone to run development."

Having the trust and understanding of senior leadership makes it much easier to secure additional resources for the development program when they are needed. "CDOs without sufficient resources to hire and support excellent staff members are bound to fail," says Jerry May, Vice President for Development at the University of Michigan. "The only way to win the resources required for a successful program is to develop and sustain a high level of credibility with organizational leaders. Developing this credibility must be among the highest priorities for new CDOs."

CDOs also need their CEOs to back them up. "When board members lose confidence in a CDO or any senior officer, they usually didn't come to that conclusion all by themselves," says Randy Helm, President of Muhlenberg College. "I try never to vent about frustrations with a cabinet member to trustees unless there is a serious problem that requires board involvement. Senior staff need to know you are holding them accountable for their performance, but also that you have their back when there are unavoidable bumps in the road."

WHEN IT'S MISSING

Lack of confidence among internal leaders in CDOs and their programs creates a host of obstacles to effective fundraising. One of the most serious repercussions of low confidence is a lack of willingness to make appropriate investments in development. Such investments include time to meet with donors and prospective donors, time to contribute to cultivation strategies, and budget support of the development staff and program.

When lack of confidence is the result of lack of CDO skill in measuring fundraising potential and designing programs to reach that potential, leaders may conclude that they need to replace the CDO. Sometimes lack of confidence might be unfounded, the result of a CEO or CFO who lacks sufficient understanding of how to support and invest appropriately in development. Either scenario carries potential to create wider lack of belief and confidence.

Lack of confidence among leaders in CDOs and other development staff members creates an environment in which fundraising becomes more and more challenging. This affects the productivity of all development staff members. If left unaddressed, such an environment will inevitably lead to the loss of strong performers who find themselves unable to do good work.

When staff members share lack of confidence in the CDO, removal of the CDO can boost confidence, provided a vacuum in leadership is addressed without delay. When they have confidence in both the CDO and the CEO but see an irreparable strain in that relationship, they generally understand the need for change and will maintain confidence provided that a remedy is not unduly delayed. When they have high confidence in the CDO and no confidence in the CEO, a CDO departure is likely to lead to destabilization and some additional staff departures.

Lack of confidence in the CDO and development program might also spread to donors and potential donors. This usually begins with board members and development volunteers, but the circle can expand quickly.

WHEN IT'S STRONG

Internal confidence in the CDO and development program, when earned and deserved, leads to appropriate investments, which make the development program more effective. Furthermore, trusted CDOs can extend the reach and impact of the CEO and enhance the effectiveness of board members. When other community members sense confidence, they are much more willing to contribute time, energy and ideas to development colleagues. And they will assist in, rather than resist, efforts to build a strong culture of philanthropic partnership.

Chapter 12

CONFIDENCE AMONG LEADERS IN THE CAPACITY TO MEET FUNDRAISING GOALS

Fundraising goals rarely decrease. They usually increase at rates greater than inflation and greater than the rate of increase expected in other revenue streams. Confidence in goals is required for success. That confidence must begin with conviction among leaders that goals are appropriately ambitious and at the same time achievable. Then the confidence must extend to staff, then volunteers, and ultimately to donors and prospective donors.

WHEN IT'S MISSING

Missed goals and unfunded projects, and even goals perceived though not yet proven to be overly ambitious and unrealistic, produce skepticism and fear and cause leaders and staff to retreat, often into a downward spiral. Such a spiral leads to less ambitious plans and less investment in the fundraising program, and these in turn lead to less engagement of donors and less fundraising revenue. Reduced confidence spreads, causing donors also to retreat or to turn their attention to other organizations.

Organizations with a history of underperformance develop excuses for their inability to raise as much as peers. These begin from a kernel of truth, but when this kernel is used to lower fundraising sights, it creates an excuse that becomes a deeply rooted, self-fulfilling prophecy. Almost every organization has excuses. Some are insidious, eating away at confidence until organizations settle for fundraising at a fraction of their potential. Others are minor, preventing fundraising in one area, or at one level. All diminish revenue.

WHEN IT'S STRONG

Strong internal confidence in the capacity to meet fundraising goals contributes to an upward spiral. Strategic planning is more ambitious, resulting in initiatives that inspire donors to make larger gifts. The perceived likelihood of projects being completed is higher, resulting in greater confidence on the part of those requesting lead gifts. Greater confidence in return on investment leads to greater investment in the fundraising program.

When it comes to excuses, staff members and volunteers at any level in an organization can make an enormous contribution simply by asking the question, "How do we know that's true?" Here are some examples of excuses that held back organizations for decades or longer, until new leadership busted them:

- A leading doctoral university: "For many years, we were a commuter school, and our campus student activity was virtually nonexistent. Our alumni never developed the kind of loyalty fostered in Ivy League schools, so they will never give at the same levels." Busting this myth, university leaders built a $30 million annual fundraising operation into a program that completed a billion-dollar campaign.

- Another leading university: "Being in the Midwest, our donors don't have the same capacity as those of eastern schools, and our alumni don't think of us as worthy of gifts in the eight-figure and nine-figure range. A gift of $1 million is a very large gift for this community." Busting this myth, university leaders built a principal gift program that converted a $150 million annual fundraising operation into a more than $400 million annual program; the main difference was a steady stream of eight-figure gifts, with occasional nine-figure gifts, on top of an already-strong program of giving at the million-dollar level and below.

- A school of music: "Our graduates are all professional musicians and educators. They don't make much money, so they won't be able to make large gifts." Ignoring this excuse, leaders found that alumni worked in many different fields, inherited wealth, married wealth, purchased real estate in major markets such as New York and Los Angeles that had appreciated considerably, bought instruments that had appreciated considerably, and otherwise had accumulated wealth sufficient to make very large gifts.

- An institute: "We don't have a natural constituency, such as alumni or subscribers, so we can't raise large gifts. We will need to rely on members who give $25 or $100." The think tank designed a council for donors of $25,000 and above whose intellectual interests were closely aligned with the institute's work. Members went on to make gifts in the seven- and eight-figure ranges, as they developed a sense of ownership of emerging initiatives.

As illustrated in numerous ways throughout this book, success breeds success. Securing one gift that runs counter to a widespread myth about diminished capacity can throw the myth into question, and multiple gifts can bust the myth altogether. Such gifts need to be highlighted. Deeply rooted excuses won't disappear overnight; persistence in fundraising in the face of these accepted "truths" and regular communication about successes are required. Naysayers may resist, having a variety of reasons to hold on to an excuse, including their own inabilities that may have led them to embrace the excuse. Using theory or benchmarking may cause some to question the prevailing "truth," but repeated success in securing gifts and in building new philanthropic partnerships exposes an excuse for what it is, permanently.

Chapter 13

BELIEF ON THE PART OF LEADERS IN PHILANTHROPIC PARTNERSHIP

Philanthropic partnership involves a donor—with ideas, expertise and financial resources—joining forces with an organization—with ideas, expertise, leadership and infrastructure—to accomplish something together that neither could accomplish without the other. This partnership requires internal belief in the partnership, expressed through readiness to come to the table as a partner, rather than a supplicant, and through willingness to engage with donors as partners, rather than simply as cash machines. In the words of not one, but dozens of major philanthropists: "I have no interest in partnering with organizations that are self-satisfied—those with leaders who have everything figured out and only want to talk with me to fund *their* plans."

Philanthropic partners are trying to get something done. They have decided to give money to nonprofit organizations and, through nonprofit organizations, to society. The question is not whether they'll give, but whether they'll give to a specific organization. Fundraisers who worry about how to separate people from their money are left in the dust by those whose principal concern is enabling philanthropists to make their biggest and best contributions to society.

Nonprofit organizations in the United States, and increasingly across the world, would not exist, and will not continue to thrive, without philanthropic partners. There is no "us and them." They are every bit as important as administrative and programmatic leaders. They provide essential financial resources, but they also provide business expertise; contribute to strategic vision; enhance visibility and reputation; and connect their organizations to many and varied constituents, ranging from potential customers (students, parents, patients, members), to civic leaders (government officials, community leaders), to other donors. Nonprofit organizations would be weaker without them, and not only financially.

Organizational representatives ready to enable philanthropy recognize that they bring just as much to the table as potential donors. They bring ideas, expertise, people, infrastructure, credibility, and a track record of accomplishment, just to name a few essential ingredients in a successful partnership.

In short, for major and transformational giving to thrive, organizational leaders must believe in the power of philanthropic partnership: They must be ready and willing to partner, and they must have the confidence and courage to work with philanthropists as partners.

WHEN IT'S MISSING

Lack of belief in philanthropic partnership may be the result of distaste for fundraising, fear of fundraising, or simply lack of understanding of how philanthropic partnership works. All of these lead to behavior that distances donors and limits the potential for major and transformational giving.

More than a few nonprofit leaders have expressed the opinion, "If only we had a large enough endowment, we wouldn't have to waste our time raising money." One university president told a colleague, "Fundraising is distasteful and beneath the dignity of this great institution." And that university, like most others in the United States, was founded and to this day is supported by prominent philanthropists! Needless to say, donors will quickly lose interest in leaders who wish they weren't around.

Those involved in fundraising, especially members of the development staff, hear it every week: "Here comes [fundraiser name here]. Hide your wallet!" Fundraisers chuckle politely, thinking to themselves how witty the speaker is to have come up with that tired line they've now heard for the 500th time. They hear it from donors, but they also hear it from colleagues, and though colleagues are usually just trying to make a joke, this and similar statements demonstrate a widespread, underlying fear of fundraising.

Fear of fundraising causes internal leaders to shy away from gift cultivation and solicitation activity. When fundraisers ask colleagues outside of development to participate in fundraising activity, the initial response will likely be, "I don't feel comfortable asking for money." Feeling that they are not in the same league as high-net-worth individuals and families, they might fear coming across as beggars, or they may simply fear that they won't know how to relate to philanthropists. Philanthropists may experience this reluctance as arrogance, sensing that leaders have made up their minds and don't need or want the input of others. Or they may experience it as lack of confidence, which in turn diminishes their own confidence in the leader, the vision or specific plans. Either way, they may feel distanced—unneeded and unwanted as partners, and wanted only as funders. They may make a gift, but it will likely be much smaller than it could have been, viewed by the donor as a transaction rather than as a partnership investment.

Even without fear or distaste, organizational leaders often lack basic understanding of philanthropic partnership. They may believe that the primary role of the fundraiser is to convince a wealthy person to part with some of his or her money, and that the person with whom the fundraiser is speaking wants to give away as little as possible. Such beliefs lead to strategies aimed at minimizing the pain, for donor as well as organizational leader. They are also seen in messaging that emphasizes the cost of giving, rather than the impact, such as messages that lead with tax benefits. Of course tax benefits are a factor, but study after study has shown that impact, pride of affiliation and many other factors are much more important to philanthropic partners.

Without belief in philanthropic partnership, internal leaders lower their own ambition. They develop strategic plans and set goals based on past fundraising performance, rather than take the risk of dreaming with a donor about what might be possible. They plan within the confines of what they consider achievable, missing opportunities that might grow from the experiences and ideas of donors.

Lowered ambition and fear of engagement with donors also combine to lead, sometimes inadvertently, to gift proposals that are fully developed before the first conversation with a potential philanthropic partner. Presenting a shiny, four-color brochure with every detail finalized may seem like proper preparation and due diligence, but it is highly likely to backfire, except in transactional, lower-level fundraising, conveying to potential major donors that there is no room for anything other than their money.

At its worst, lack of belief in philanthropic partnership on the part of organizational leaders—whether out of distaste, fear or lack of understanding—is accompanied by a sense of entitlement; leaders act and even speak as though a board member or other involved person "owes" them a gift. Solicitations for large gifts outside of the context of a strong partnership can easily convey arrogance, if not desperation. A colleague told the story of a chief development officer and president so desperate for a large naming gift that they ignored the advice of numerous colleagues—not to mention their own gut instincts—and threw a "Hail Mary" pass at one of their most generous donors. The request was completely outside of the donor's area of interest. Furthermore, the donor was well known to have little interest in naming gifts. The answer was an immediate and unsurprising "no."

WHEN IT'S STRONG

The Comer Children's Hospital at the University of Chicago is a powerful example of philanthropic partnership. "My wife Francie and I have been determined to find the most effective ways to give back to my old neighborhood. We have chosen to do that by focusing on fundamental needs, such as children's health and education. What could be more important than that?" (University of Chicago Medicine, 2006). With these words, Gary Comer, founder of the Land's End clothing empire, expressed an idea, a vision, a philanthropic objective. Their gifts to the neighborhood included the Comer Youth Center, gifts for the Revere School and support of neighborhood housing initiatives. Though not graduates of the University of Chicago, they accomplished this objective in large measure through partnership with the university, which is located in Gary's old neighborhood. They gave $21 million to build the hospital, then $20 million to add a pediatric emergency room, then $42 million to expand the hospital and add a Center for Children and Specialty Care. Their gifts were not so much gifts *to* the University of Chicago as *through* the University of Chicago to the neighborhood. The university had an established medical center with infrastructure and leadership that allowed the Comers to accomplish their own objectives in a highly effective way. The Comers and the university accomplished something together that neither could have done nearly as effectively without the other.

"Informed philanthropists are not interlopers, in most situations," says Charles Wall. "They can be highly effective partners. Organizations should encourage potential partners by asking them to call to their attention things they think the organizations should consider doing. If these potential partners take the time to suggest initiatives, they're probably going to be interested in funding them."

Openness to philanthropic partnership on the part of organization leaders produces, in the words of one leading philanthropist, "a space in which major donors more readily voice their own philanthropic objectives, fully aware that their offer of an idea conveys an offer to fund the idea." In this space, in the words of one university president with a long track record of eight- and nine-figure gifts, "Some donors will respond to another person's idea by saying, 'I want to do exactly *that*,' while other donors may respond to the context of ambition and achievement, rather than another person's idea, and offer, 'I want to do something like *this*.'" When organizational leaders take the time to listen, engage and educate, their strategic objectives and the objectives of philanthropists come into alignment, and everyone benefits.

THE ULTIMATE EXPRESSION OF PARTNERSHIP

The principal beneficiaries named in wills are family members, close friends and charitable interests. "When donors include organizations in their estate plans, they have elevated those organizations to the status of family member," says Robert Sharpe, president of the Sharpe Group and a widely recognized expert in gift planning. Organizational representatives who are notified of a donor's bequest intention should consider how they would treat a relative who just notified them of a bequest and be guided by this consideration. In many cases, these donors are tying their legacy to an organization, through creating or adding to an endowment that bears their name, or the name of someone they wish to honor, in perpetuity. In most other cases, they allow the organization to use the funds in an unrestricted way, an ultimate expression of confidence in the organization and its future. In all cases, they have included the organization in their last will and testament, one of their final expressions of who and what was important to them in this world and worthy of perpetuating.

"Being named in a will can be the result of a direct request, but more often it results from donors' decisions about how they would like their life's accumulate assets to be used philanthropically," adds Robert Sharpe. "And these decisions can sometimes be influenced by the example of other donors. Being retained and named in the *last* will, however—the only will that matters—is earned, whether or not it is ever actively solicited." Naming a nonprofit organization as the beneficiary of an estate is an ultimate expression of partnership.

Section III

FACILITATORS: STAFF AND VOLUNTEERS— DEVELOPMENT AND BEYOND

Chapter 14

STAFF AND VOLUNTEER
BELIEF IN MISSION

Those working most directly on fundraising activity—development staff and volunteers—play one of the most critical roles in reinforcing overall donor and leader belief and confidence. Staff outside of development and in every part of an organization also contribute to or diminish belief and confidence, and many of them have little appreciation for the power they have in this regard. For all these staff members and volunteers, personal belief in an organization's mission allows them to be much more effective in these contributions. Not surprisingly, it also contributes to satisfaction with their work and longevity of service.

STAFF IN DEVELOPMENT

As the development profession has grown, and as the competition for talented and experienced fundraisers has intensified, the opportunities for the best and brightest fundraising professionals have exploded. This has led to an increase in candidates chasing salary and title and in hiring managers focusing on performance measures such as number and size of gifts "raised" (as if any individual fundraiser is entirely responsible for a gift, but that subject requires another book), often at the expense of candidate and hiring manager focus on mission alignment.

Individuals with deep personal commitment to the mission of their organizations and whose commitment to mission is recognized and valued by their supervisors are much more likely to stay. This mission alignment adds a perhaps intangible but nevertheless powerful benefit to their overall compensation "package."

Furthermore, philanthropists want to engage with fundraising staff who share their passion. When asked about development officers with whom they've worked, every philanthropist has a story of a staff member who lacked this belief, and another story of a favorite development officer whose own commitment to mission made them excited to be a part of the organization. It should come as no surprise that the ones invited to dinner parties, and the ones with whom philanthropists stay in touch for years and sometimes decades after their initial relationship centered in a specific organization, are in the latter category.

Those charged with hiring development officers shouldn't settle for individuals who don't excite their own passion for their organizations, reminding them of why they joined their organizations as a staff member or volunteer in the first place.

VOLUNTEERS

Volunteers generally bring strong belief in an organization's mission. The importance of this belief is included here not so much to suggest that volunteers might lack this belief as to point out that fundraising programs don't benefit from volunteer belief *unless they have volunteers!* Chapter 25 discusses in greater detail the importance of involving potential philanthropic partners as volunteers.

Volunteer belief carries a different weight than belief on the part of paid staff. Volunteers aren't being paid, and they are asking potential donors to do something they themselves are doing—voluntarily giving of their precious time and financial resources. Through their demonstrated belief, volunteers give confidence to others in their position—social peers, business peers, giving peers. Organizations that raise large and transformational gifts tend to raise more large and transformational gifts, and one key factor in this snowball effect is the belief conveyed by those who have already done what is being asked.

STAFF IN EVERY PART OF
THE ORGANIZATION

One of the most important tasks of CEOs, chief development officers and development staff is to educate staff throughout an organization on the role they play in building belief and confidence. As with development staff, the more they share a belief in mission, the more effective they will be in that role.

WHEN IT'S MISSING

When staff member belief in mission is missing, donors experience giving in a much more transactional way, unable to share their own passion with the staff member with whom they are working.

For staff members, the work is so much more laborious, and the reward is more shallow. Given the temptation of title and compensation, it is not unusual for fundraisers in particular, but also staff members in other parts of nonprofit organizations, to take one career step away from their true passion or passions, convincing themselves that they will develop passion for the new organization. Sometimes that works, but usually it does not, and fundraisers find themselves yearning to get back to the type of organization that rewards them on a deeper level.

WHEN IT'S STRONG

"The best nonprofit managers and staff members I've known have a deep, personal connection with an organization's mission," says philanthropist Joan Harris. "They relate, intimately, to the passion of board members, volunteers and donors, and this results in much more effective fundraising."

"My personal belief in the missions of the organizations I've served has sustained and inspired me in this work for over 30 years," says Rebecca Tseng Smith, associate dean, external relations, Stanford Graduate School of Education, and chair of the annual CASE conference, Inspiring the Largest Gifts of a Lifetime. "I've met so many wonderful people—both colleagues and donors; many of them have become lifelong friends. Our shared love of our organizations has rewarded me far beyond whatever I've been paid. I look back on all these years with great pride in my connection and the part I've played in helping great organizations do important work."

Chapter 15

STAFF AND VOLUNTEER CONFIDENCE IN LEADERS, PLANS AND GOALS

Staff members and volunteers are an organization's army, when it comes to fundraising. The board may have 40 members, and the senior administration a handful who are deeply engaged in fundraising, but staff and volunteers number in the dozens if not hundreds or thousands. Behind every successful fundraising effort one finds a leader, and usually several, who excel in inspiring confidence in others.

Staff members and volunteers rely on these leaders not only to provide inspiration but also to shape exciting yet strategic plans and to set ambitious yet achievable goals related to those plans. All elements are important—they may find leaders to be inspirational, and they may be excited by plans and ambitious goals, but they need also to have confidence that plans are *strategic* and goals are *achievable*.

WHEN IT'S MISSING

Staff members, especially the most talented and skilled, are in high demand. Many of those in fundraising work are highly driven and competitive, and they will seek out leaders who allow them to reach and surpass ambitious personal goals. Volunteers have dozens of opportunities to give time, talent and treasure, and loss of confidence in leaders can be enough to shift their attention to other organizations.

Development staff members and volunteers are on the front line, and they will in many cases be answering questions about the details of plans and goals. When front-line fundraisers don't understand or don't have confidence, they are less able to convey confidence to potential donors.

Staff beyond the development office will also, in some cases, be talking directly with donors. In more cases, they will be responsible for implementing plans, ensuring success in initiatives, measuring impact and reporting on that impact to donors, either directly or through their development colleagues. Leaders play an important role, to be sure, but staff members make projects happen, and potential philanthropic partners know that. When staff members don't have confidence in their leaders or in an organization's overall direction, it shows, and it can diminish donor confidence.

WHEN IT'S STRONG

Confidence-inspiring leaders may be found on the board; in the president's chair; on the executive team; in the ranks of the faculty, physicians or musicians; and in many other parts of an organization. As I discussed in *The Chief Development Officer: Beyond Fundraising,* organizations increasingly rely on chief development officers to boost confidence internally and externally. Some leaders excel in inspiring large groups, and others are more effective in the context of strong one-to-one relationships built over time. They play a critical role in creating environments in which all can and do contribute to their fullest potential. They also create and reinforce the sense of a winning team. The more they are in number, the more broadly and deeply belief and confidence are felt. They give staff members and volunteers the energy they need to charge ahead, advancing the organization, and they rally the troops when inevitable challenges arise and lulls in fundraising progress occur.

Successful leaders inspire followership. Just as successful fundraisers engage donors as partners, successful leaders engage staff members and volunteers as willing and eager followers and partners, personally invested in the leader's and the organization's success. Followers depend on integrity, transparency, consensus, appropriate levels of support, vision, compelling plans, ambitious but achievable goals, and inspiration. When leaders provide these, followers know they will achieve something important and even extraordinary and that they will derive pride from their association with the organization.

"The most successful leader I've ever known and worked for was able to support staff emotionally and persuasively toward a common goal," says fundraising professional Carmen Creel. "Working hard toward that goal was always fun; people were never trudging. He consistently and publicly celebrated group achievement, recognizing and thanking every member of the team when a goal was achieved or surpassed. He was authentic in his relationships with everyone, so team members always felt heard; we always felt important in his presence. These qualities inspired all of us to work even harder, to feel more invested and to feel a sense of ownership in final outcomes."

When those doing front-line work are deeply knowledgeable about plans and goals, they are much more confident and much more likely to succeed in engaging the confidence of potential donors. "Confidence in our organization's leaders and knowledge about strategies, including knowledge gained from some involvement in shaping those strategies, have prepared us well for fielding calls from donors who have questions and concerns," says Alex Brose, vice president for development at the Aspen Music Festival and School. "More importantly, they have allowed us to *reach out* to donors more proactively, asking them to partner with us on a path and with a team that everyone can get behind."

Successful organizations clearly and regularly communicate widely about goals and plans, in order to instill confidence in all staff members and volunteers. This communication comes from leaders but also from key executors, demonstrating consensus and resulting in even wider consensus that goals are appropriately ambitious and achievable. When staff members and volunteers in every part of an organization understand and embrace plans and goals, their confidence has a positive impact on others around them, expanding on the confidence inspired by the development staff.

Regular reporting on *progress* also sustains confidence and builds momentum. People understand roadblocks and setbacks, and they do not lose confidence when they are told about, and believe in, plans to overcome obstacles. Success breeds success, but not if people don't know about it! In fundraising, there is always a new and higher goal to reach, and successful organizations and leaders celebrate successes along the way. These celebrations not only recognize excellent work; they also build confidence that more success lies ahead.

Chapter 16

STAFF AND VOLUNTEER BELIEF THAT INDIVIDUAL CONTRIBUTIONS MAKE A DIFFERENCE

As discussed in the past few chapters, mission alignment, confidence in leaders, and confidence in plans and goals contribute to effectiveness, satisfaction, and longevity of service of staff members and volunteers. These in turn contribute to overall levels of belief and confidence throughout an organization. But belief that individual contributions make a difference is also critically important. The larger an organization, the harder this belief can be to maintain.

In small organizations, most staff members, and even volunteers, wear multiple hats. Direct interaction with leaders, front-line workers, and individuals served by the organization is also much more likely and frequent. Staff members and volunteers have more opportunities, generally speaking, to see the direct impact of their work. With staffing usually lean, they and their colleagues will notice the effects of one person's absence or weak contribution. Conversely, everybody knows when a high performer joins the team.

In large organizations, development officers may be, or at least feel, several layers removed from impact. Those working in prospect research, for example, may never hear about the results of a meeting between the president and a new prospective donor identified by the research team. Major gift officers, traveling frequently, may never meet the faculty members or students who benefit from their work. As development departments grow, many organizations have relocated staff members to offices off campus, down the street from the hospital or to an office building a mile away from the orchestra hall.

In large organizations, staff members can also feel siloed, focused in one area of expertise, but without a sense of how their area fits into the department as a whole, let alone the organization as a whole.

In organizations large and small, the tremendous responsibilities of CEOs and chief development officers related to the board, financial and strategic planning, fundraising, government relations, and so on, in the context of a highly competitive environment, leave little time for engagement with the full staff and with volunteers beyond the board.

With these forces at work in combination, it is easy to see how staff members, volunteers who are not on the board, and sometimes even board members who are not on the executive committee can lose sight of the big picture, feel disconnected from mission fulfillment, and lose confidence that their individual contributions really make a difference.

WHEN IT'S MISSING

When staff members lose confidence that their contribution is noticed and matters, they look for new managers or even new organizations. In my work in search, lack of this confidence comes up much more often than dissatisfaction with level of authority or compensation, for those who are looking to make a change.

WHEN IT'S STRONG

When confidence is strong, retention is easier and longevity improves. Staff satisfaction and morale is higher for the individual. This spills over into stronger teamwork and team satisfaction. Volunteers and donors notice as well, and all these factors combine to create an upward spiral in fundraising results.

Section IV

PHILANTHROPIST TO PHILANTHROPIST

Chapter 17

PHILANTHROPIST TO PHILANTHROPIST: FIND YOUR PASSION

Every philanthropist interviewed identified passion for the mission as one of the most important factors in determining satisfaction in any given major or transformational giving experience. Most ranked it as the most important.

"There are so many good causes, so many problems that could be solved if resources were there," says philanthropist Constance Keller. "You must look at that universe and see what speaks to you. In our view, it is more satisfying to concentrate on the two or three things you find most important. By concentrating you will learn, and you will be invited to serve, and by serving you will learn more. This learning is not only enjoyable, it will also illuminate your decision-making as to where you'll get the best societal return on your philanthropic investment."

"Most nonprofit leaders genuinely care about their work, and most of their ideas are good ideas," adds Mellody Hobson. "But you, as a philanthropist, can't get everything done. Stay focused on the issues that move you."

"Whatever people say to you about the project they are pitching, they will make it sound exciting," says Adrienne Arsht. "But their plans will inevitably involve having you fix something. Take your time. If you aren't ready, say you aren't taking on any projects at this time (say 'at this time' rather than 'this year,' otherwise you'll be encouraging another visit next year!). As you explore options, you'll start to see what things are most meaningful to you, and you'll make more informed decisions about where to allocate your limited time and financial resources."

"Make sure it's something that reaches your heart," adds Ann Ziff. "You're going to feel pressure from friends and colleagues, but make sure what you do strikes a chord for you. Start by giving a little time, or a small gift, and determine if it's emotionally *and* intellectually satisfying."

"For me, it's all about education," says philanthropist Ann Korologos. "I am passionate about educational organizations, but I also want to continue to learn. In our philanthropy, we are fortunate to work with organizations that allow us to grow even as we help others to grow."

"I spend a lot of time with philanthropists who say they want to be anonymous," says Jason Franklin. "Often, what they truly want is to avoid being hounded by other nonprofits as a result of their gift. Over time, those focused on anonymity for this reason learn that active givers instead learn to say 'no.' When they learn how to do so, they free themselves to say 'yes' in a way that's incredibly exciting and fulfilling."

"Philanthropy has the potential to unlock a deeply felt interest or passion," says philanthropist Chris Denby. "Don't support organizations only out of a sense of duty or a desire to do good, because those causes might not be the things that truly animate you. Philanthropy helps us complete our lives and opens doors to whole new worlds of excitement."

"I like to talk about the organizations I support," says Ann Friedman. "When I'm passionate, I get more involved, and when I'm involved, I learn things that feed my passion. The more I learn, the more knowledgeable I am when discussing my work with family members and friends."

Passion increases enjoyment in asking others to become involved. "When I'm passionate about a project, I don't mind fundraising at all," says philanthropist Nancy Magoon. And passion can be contagious. "It's important to let other people see your passion," continues Nancy. "As our success in fundraising for the Aspen Art Museum grew, one couple approached me, asking why we hadn't asked them. They wanted to be a part of it!"

"Know what you want to do," says philanthropist Jim Crown. "The idea doesn't have to come from you. But you really need to buy into the objective. Then know how your gift will achieve the objective."

Finding your passion can and should include thoughtful exploration. "Begin with research," says philanthropist Lynda Resnick. "Take the time to determine what's most important to you in life. Allow people to come to you, and go out and listen. You may find people pursuing ideas that are new and compelling to you. Once you know where you want to invest your philanthropic dollars, get to know organizations with missions that align with your objectives, and listen to their leaders. Don't assume you know what they most need. You wouldn't launch a business without careful research; apply the same approach to your philanthropy."

"Give to your passion, or you will likely be disappointed in the outcome," says philanthropist Tim Gill. "Become an expert in your field of interest so you know what you want," he adds. "Give in a way that's unique—don't just give the same way everyone else does. You can be creative in ways that others can't."

"Passion will give you the strength to persevere," says Adrienne Arsht. "Without passion, it can feel a bit like quicksand—easy to get in, hard to get out, and you'll be miserable." In other cases, passion may outstrip an organization's ambition or capacity. "Make sure the passion of your foot isn't larger than the shoe of the organization," she adds. "Otherwise, you'll be in excruciating pain!"

Chapter 18

PHILANTHROPIST TO PHILANTHROPIST: FIND YOUR PARTNER

"Once you know what you want to do, don't just say 'yes' to the first person who knocks on your door," says philanthropist Leonard Lauder. "Think, think, think. Ask yourself, 'Are they looking to solve a great problem or to keep themselves employed? Will they help you change people's lives, or will you just be one of many keeping the organization or the development department alive? Will the organization survive without you?' It's hard to know all the right questions, but start by asking yourself these, and many more questions will follow. Eventually, you'll find the answers that give you the confidence you've found the right organizations and the right leaders—the right partners to help you get done what you most want to do."

"Before making a major gift, get to know the organization and its leadership well," says philanthropist Mercedes Bass. "Unless someone at the top agrees with what you're doing, you'll fail," adds Adrienne Arsht. "Find out early if the president and board chair are on your wavelength."

"You don't have to reinvent the wheel," says Mellody Hobson. "Business leaders know that buying an existing product or service is sometimes better business practice than building something new. In their philanthropy, however, they too often think they have to start from scratch. Philanthropists should look for existing organizations and leaders who share their passion and vision—there are many already doing great work."

When a philanthropist is initiating an idea, he or she should test the idea with several potential partners, finding the organization that most closely shares the same passion, is best positioned to execute it to its fullest potential, and is committed to making it a priority. "When I moved from Miami to Washington, D.C., I began talking with friends and colleagues all over town about the need for a center focused on Latin America," says Adrienne Arsht. "Fred Kempe, president and CEO of the Atlantic Council, listened. He and the board came to me, saying that they would like to build upon my vision and passion and create a center that would integrate Latin America with Europe and the United States, replacing outdated perceptions and visions of the region and creating new opportunities for engagement and mutual influence. I started with a small contribution to fund a study, so we could together confirm the need and determine the viability of the project. The need was confirmed, and I gave the gift that established the center. Atlantic Council has been the perfect partner. Within the first year alone, we had 50 events in eight cities, we developed eight regional and thematic initiatives, we produced 15 publications, we had over 2,000 mentions and opinion pieces in U.S. and international media, and we created 13 new partnerships. One of our publications on U.S.-Cuba relations played an instrumental role in the historic policy change announced by President Obama in December 2014, opening diplomatic relations, facilitating trade and expanding travel. It's thrilling to see how much impact we've been able to have, together, in such a short time!"

"We had a code name for our work with Adrienne Arsht," says Fred Kempe. "We called it the 'Lindsey Vonn project.' We even had an artist do a rendering of Adrienne on a downhill course navigating all obstacles. We had met an irrepressible philanthropist, a business entrepreneur who was determined to make a social and political difference of some significance, changing the very way we understood Latin America and interacted with an entire continent. Her vision was that Latin America should be brought into the broader Atlantic community and that policy makers too often neglected our closest neighbors. She thinks out of the box. She worked with us to land the most impressive director we could have found, a true social entrepreneur. And she demands quality in all aspects of performance. Yet she never touches the intellectual independence and creative license that makes the Atlantic Council sparkle. There's not a week that she doesn't provide me an insight or suggestion that helps advance the center or the Atlantic Council more broadly."

Philanthropists seek partners who are accountable. "Find a partner who ascribes to your vision and values, who brings the most innovative ideas to the discussion, and who can carry it through," says Jeanette Lerman-Neubauer. "The right leader wants the right donor partner, and vice versa. Then measure, or you won't know if you've arrived."

Philanthropist Paula Crown agrees. "Financial support in any area should rely on more than vague intangibles." A longtime advocate for the arts—she serves on the President's Committee on the Arts and the Humanities—she uses arts as an example: "Engagement in the arts has been proven to enhance academic outcomes, inspire professional success and change communities. There is no reason why metrics and evidence-based objectives can't be part of philanthropy in the arts."

"There are many worthy causes, and well-constructed messages can produce an immediate and powerful emotional response," says Jim Crown. "But sometimes a little logic takes you from a fast-beating heart to a conclusion that 'this won't work.' It's tempting to follow a charismatic person, or to follow someone else who puts a lot of their own money into a project. Take time for critical review of the strategy, lest you make a gift that doesn't work and that you'll later regret."

Even when a trusted relationship and clear measures are firmly in place, philanthropic partners deserve and usually expect engagement in the planning process. "We initiated the idea, and we asked Mark Siegler to figure out how to do it and what it would cost," says philanthropist Kay Bucksbaum, describing what would become the Bucksbaum Institute for Clinical Excellence at the University of Chicago. "Every step in the planning was reviewed by me, my children, our attorney and the administration of the University of Chicago. We had confidence in the leaders, and, by mutual engagement throughout the process, we had well-placed confidence in the project."

Philanthropists also encourage emerging philanthropists to aim for long-term relationships with organizational partners. "Once you find leaders who share your passion and organizations that allow you to have the impact you want to have, stay with them, and build on your giving," says Mercedes Bass. "Your giving will lead to more involvement, and more involvement will lead to a greater desire to give. Increased giving, in turn, will lead to greater impact and deeper satisfaction."

Sometimes, an idea will involve multiple partners. "Several years ago, we initiated the idea of a digitization project," says Leonard Polonsky. "My objective was democratizing access to information, enabling people across the globe to view documents that were previously very difficult to access. The Polonsky Foundation's first partners were Cambridge University Library, with whom we digitized fragments of the Cairo Genizah and the papers of Sir Isaac Newton, and the Hebrew University of Jerusalem, with whom we digitized their Albert Einstein Archives. We then created a collaboration between two of the greatest library collections in the world: the Bodleian of the University of Oxford and the Biblioteca Apostolica Vaticana (Vatican Library). Both the project and the collaboration itself were groundbreaking. Our partners have also included the Jewish Theological Seminary, the British Library, the Library of Congress and the New York Public Library, among others. Twenty-first-century technology provides the opportunity for new collaborations and for new ways of managing and disseminating information, knowledge and expertise to scholars and to the general public worldwide. Bringing this idea to fruition has involved a great deal of time, effort and financial support, and it has been one of the most gratifying experiences of our lives."

As illustrated above, philanthropic partners enjoy creating partnerships among nonprofit organizations. While sitting on the board of a health network and the largest medical center in Canada, Sandra Rotman saw an opportunity to apply business skills to collective buying and more efficient use of government funds. She and her husband, Joseph, who had transformed the reach and impact of the University of Toronto School of Management that bears his name, created a chair at the business school that grew into a center for health sector strategy. Today, it is an internationally renowned center on which the government relies for policy development. "Joe believed in extending the impact of philanthropy through building intellectual bridges," says Sandy.

The Rotmans also created Rise Asset Development. In collaboration with the Center for Addiction and Mental Health and the Rotman School of Management, Rise provides microfinancing and mentorship to entrepreneurs living with mental health and addiction challenges. "Sometimes all that someone needs is a mentor, a little bit of financial support and a vote of confidence," says Sandy Rotman. "And we change people's lives. I'm very proud of that. We now have government support and corporate support, and we're working to take this program across Canada."

Successful philanthropic partnership might also require partners beyond nonprofit organizations. "Collaboration has been a critical component of our success in multiple philanthropic endeavors," says Bill Budinger. "In Key West, our partners in both the public and private sector have enabled us to build capacity within existing and new entities, creating self-sustaining arts venues that have established national and even international reputations. Our work in the Delaware school system has brought together the business community, the teachers' union, and others to reduce polarization and contention, resulting in improved test scores and first-place awards in the first and second phases of Race to the Top. With the right people at the table, philanthropy has great power to leverage change."

"John and I invest primarily in organizations that deal with systemic change and are highly scalable," adds philanthropist Ann Doerr. "Whether in education, climate or any number of other areas, philanthropy can only go so far. Philanthropists and nonprofit leaders need additional partners who can affect policy and extend impact. For example, the Environmental Defense Fund worked with the state of California to initiate the nation's first economy-wide cap on greenhouse gases, and with FedEx to develop a delivery truck that reduced soot emissions by 90 percent. Major national and global issues are complex; solutions will involve many partners."

Philanthropic partnership that leads to transformational giving is possible with a finite number of organizations. That number varies according to the type and degree of involvement desired by the philanthropist. Yet philanthropists usually have a larger number of organizations they want to support, at least at some level. "I recommend a 50/30/20 rule," says Jason Franklin. "Set aside 50 percent of your philanthropic dollars for no more than three organizations. Have the discipline to pick the two or three that excite you the most and allow you to have the biggest impact in the world. Make these your partners. Get involved, and leverage your networks for further support. Set aside 30 percent for other organizations you want to support, but not in a transformational way. And set aside 20 percent for 'impulse' giving—giving to organizations and friends to whom you simply want to say 'yes,' or for giving in response to a disaster or event that especially inspires you. The percentages may vary, but this approach frees donors from becoming trapped in the middle, where they feel obliged to support everybody and yet support nobody in a transformational way."

Chapter 19

PHILANTHROPIST TO PHILANTHROPIST: GET INVOLVED

"My giving is intimately intertwined with my involvement," says Chris Denby. "Usually, I'm on the board or otherwise deeply involved. My gift is therefore only a part of my overall contribution to transformation." Sandra Rotman agrees. "Joe's father taught us that money is the easy part," she says. "My husband and I took his father's advice to heart, recognizing that successful philanthropists are those who give time in addition to money and who have an ability to create collaboration that drives transformation."

"The most rewarding work in philanthropy is done hands on rather than at arms' length," adds Mellody Hobson. "It's nice to put on a pretty dress and attend a gala, but getting close to the work is what makes a giving experience truly satisfying. When you're involved, you see and understand the impact more clearly. Perhaps more important, you also care more and feel a much bigger sense of responsibility."

"Sometimes, your biggest gift is not the money," says Bill Budinger. "In my own philanthropy, there have been many times when my focus and my commitment in the face of obstacles were more important than the money. And being committed is the reason I get out of bed. I love to fish. But given the projects in which I'm involved, I haven't been fishing in four years! And I'm happy with that."

"I can't emphasize enough the importance of rolling up your sleeves and participating, coming to understand really well the institutions that are doing the things you think are most important," says Dennis Keller. "That participation will lead to relationships with the people who will steward your gifts, allowing them to understand and make happen what you hope will happen as a result of your gifts."

"The most precious asset we have is time," says Raymond J. McGuire. "The most substantive and the most rewarding philanthropy involves giving time, together with ideas, financial resources, and outreach to personal and professional networks on behalf of an organization. My largest gifts have gone hand in hand with involvement as a leader and contributions to vision, strategy, and direct support of the chief executive."

For these and other reasons, many philanthropists prefer to wait on major and transformational giving until they have time for involvement. "It's OK to delay major gift giving until you're ready to be involved," says Peter Meinig. "Write a smaller check, meet people in the organization, and find out whether the organization is one where you really want to devote your time and expertise." "If you're leading an organization," adds Nancy Meinig, "give people who are still building careers, raising families and building wealth time to get to know your organization. Don't rush major giving. Have patience, be good stewards and stay in touch."

GOVERNING BOARD SERVICE

"Being on a board is a responsibility," says Charles Wall. "It takes time and commitment. As a fellow board member recently said, 'It's not just to add a line to your obituary!' If you take this responsibility seriously, the resulting relationship makes giving much more rewarding. That's why I've kept the number of boards on which I serve reasonably small, so I can enjoy that depth of relationship."

"Look for boards that have attracted people you respect and have engaged them in meaningful ways," says Ann Korologos. "Make sure you enjoy the other board members, because you should be spending a lot of time with them," adds Adrienne Arsht. "If you do join a board, go to the meetings," adds Ann Friedman. "Be involved. Ask your questions, even if it's intimidating. Only by asking will you understand where you can add value."

"Board membership means leading from the front, when it comes to giving," says Robert Hurst. "When we are serving in a leadership role and we see a need, we step forward without waiting to be asked," adds Soledad Hurst.

An invitation to join a governing board can be flattering, but philanthropists urge emerging philanthropists to avoid saying "yes" without some due diligence. "Early in my philanthropy, I joined a board and made a $10 million gift without taking time to get to know the organization's board and management well," says one philanthropist. "What a mistake I made! I felt I needed to lead and set a standard. But I said 'yes' before doing proper background work. I've learned that philanthropy is a partnership, and I need to evaluate readiness for partnership—on my part and on the part of the organization—just as carefully as I would in approaching a potential business partner, or in considering an investment in a company. Philanthropy is serious business. You should have fun, and it can be very rewarding, but it is not something you do on the fly."

OTHER WAYS TO BE INVOLVED

Governing board membership is only one of many ways to get involved. Advisory boards, task forces, visiting committees and other groups offer a variety of ways to be engaged. "Through the Ravinia Women's Board, I've been involved in a student orchestra program in the public schools," says philanthropist Becky Murray. "I love seeing children's faces light up when they are handed instruments. One little girl was asked how she felt when she got her instrument. 'I was like a volcano, waiting to explode!' she exclaimed. Seeing this project flourish firsthand has made our giving so much more rewarding."

For some donors, involvement with recipients is at least as important as, if not more important than, involvement in governance or even involvement in a formal group. "Involvement opportunities should be tailored to a donor's personal style," says Jim Crown. "For us, the most important aspect of involvement related to a gift is periodic engagement with those who are doing the work, so we truly understand what the gift is achieving."

"One of my best philanthropic experiences has been supporting low-income children who need a little extra help to realize the dream of attending college," adds John Fullerton. "Our money is important, but the most rewarding part has been getting to know the kids through mentoring. One of the hardest-working kids I've ever met, whose parents only finished elementary school, is now headed to Duke. That drive is so important in life, and it is a great joy to help young people who have it."

Section V

FACILITATORS: WHAT CAN I DO?

Chapter 20

START WITH THE DONOR

Every day, in organizations throughout the world, staff members and even volunteers sit in prospect strategy sessions, crafting cultivation and solicitation strategies, and often arguing over who gets to ask a donor, how much they get to request, and what giving opportunities should be presented. Everyone who has sat in on such a discussion knows which voice is usually missing: the voice of the donor.

When major institutional leaders who have relationships with donors are bickering over whose program the donor "should" be asked to support, *ask the donor!*

"In preparing for our last campaign, one couple, because of their history of support, appeared on the prospective donor lists of seven different areas of the university," says Connie Kravas, vice president for university advancement and president of the University of Washington Foundation. "Clearly, this worried us! We wanted to be respectful of these incredibly philanthropic donors, so we went to them, at the outset, not to ask for a gift, but to seek their guidance."

"We were open and honest," she continues. "'Because of your history of generosity, it may not surprise you that there are many areas of the university that view you as their closest friends and donors,' we told them. 'We are not here to ask for a gift, but rather to ask for your counsel. Should you choose to make additional contributions during the campaign ahead, we want it to be a truly magnificent experience for you.' Then we listened."

"The couple found the honesty of this approach both appealing and authentic. It led to a clear statement of what they wanted to support and when and how each of the seven programs should approach them. Rather than having a negative reaction to competition among different parts of the university, they felt totally in control. They relished the feeling of being treated as thoughtful partners. That experience was so enlightening that we now ask many of our most generous donors, 'When's the right time to ask? What's the right ask?'"

Fundraisers in doubt about the best way to proceed in a cultivation or solicitation strategy should go and see the donor. Fundraisers who have lost perspective on why they're working for an organization should go and see donors. Fundraisers who have lost their joy in the profession need to go and talk with donors. In short, everyone involved in fundraising stands to benefit from more time with donors!

Chapter 21

DON'T CHASE
WEALTHY PEOPLE FIRST—
FIND PHILANTHROPISTS!

Major and transformational giving requires wealth. For some organizations, major and transformational gifts will be measured in the thousands of dollars, and for others, in the millions or tens of millions. But these gifts will come from those with the capacity to make them. Hence, a fundraiser's first and reasonable instinct is to identify those who have that capacity.

But capacity is not enough. Some wealthy people are not and will never be philanthropic. Others will delay giving until later in life: Some will wait until they have finished building a business, and others will wait until they have provided for their family. Some will delay philanthropy in order to give it the same level of care and attention that they gave to building their wealth. Fundraisers should plant seeds with all, allowing for the possibility of a major or transformative gift years or decades in the future. But fundraisers should focus time and energy first on philanthropists—people who have made clear through word and deed that they are interested in giving a portion of their money to nonprofit organizations.

Instead of asking, "Who has a lot of money?" fundraisers seeking philanthropic partners ask, "Who *gives* a lot of money?" Nonprofit leaders—both paid professionals and volunteers—spend enormous amounts of time in nominating committee meetings, development committee meetings, campaign planning meetings and prospect management discussions looking at wealth screenings and creating strategies designed to separate someone from some of that wealth. Too little attention is paid to those already giving. In the case of those giving to the organization, the focus needs to be on factors that would elevate the institution's priority in their overall giving. In the case of those giving to other institutions, the focus should be on understanding the donors' philanthropic priorities and determining whether any of these align, or might align, with the institution's strategic objectives.

Among those already giving to an organization, one often-neglected group is consistent donors whose giving flies under the radar. They may have given to an organization for 20 or 30 years, but because they have not made a high-level gift, they have gone unnoticed. Despite receiving the same, usually impersonal solicitation letter each year, perhaps with a few sentences rearranged or updated, these loyal donors have raised their hand time and time again. Some will never form the donative intent to make that organization a priority in their giving, but many have substantially greater capacity that may go undiscovered without personal contact.

Visits with loyal, consistent donors are often among the easiest to arrange and the most enjoyable. Wise gift officers sprinkle in a meeting or two with a consistent donor—someone who has given for 25 years, for example, even if his or her largest gift has been $100. They find that longevity and consistency often indicate high levels of belief and confidence that, combined with deeper engagement, might well lead to substantially increased giving.

Early in my career, I visited with a donor who had given small amounts every year since she graduated, a giving record that spanned more than 30 years. She listed her occupation as "piano teacher." This was before the days when the Internet vastly expanded research capabilities. An international address and a foreign name further restricted our research efforts, so we knew little about this "piano teacher" until my colleague and I met her in person, a meeting designed simply to thank her for her consistent support. We found we were meeting with a great philanthropist with extremely high capacity, actively building schools and improving education in her native hometown halfway around the globe from her alma mater. She and her husband were investing millions of dollars and deriving great joy from these projects. By paying attention to consistency of giving, and not merely amount, we found one of our highest-capacity prospective donors.

Today's technology, and the increased sophistication of prospect development professionals, make it much easier to identify both wealth and a demonstrated philanthropic nature. It is a lot easier to engage a philanthropist in giving than a wealthy person who does not have charitable intent, regardless of the extent of that person's wealth.

Chapter 22

PAY ATTENTION TO
PHILANTHROPIC PRIORITY

Most fundraising programs rate prospective donors according to giving capacity and giving inclination. Giving *capacity* ratings are based on total known net worth: If a prospective-donor couple is known to have $100 million, they might be rated $5 million, meaning that they are considered able to make a gift of $5 million paid over a five-year campaign period. Giving *inclination* ratings are based on a gift officer's assessment of current willingness and readiness to make a gift to the institution: If one member of the couple is a board member, or if the couple has a long history of giving or has told the institution that they are planning to make a gift, their inclination rating is likely to be "high." If they have expressed dissatisfaction with the institution's plans or leadership, they might be rated "low."

Giving capacity ratings are critically important. Development officers and prospect researchers continuously gather information that contributes to more and more accurate ratings, from public sources, friends and colleagues of prospective donors, and from prospective donors themselves. Prospective donors, of course, have the best information about their own wealth, and the closer they become to the institution, the more likely they are to share such information.

Inclination ratings are less widely used and more subjective, unless the rating comes directly from the prospective donor, and even then the information may lead to inaccurate projections. Donors may have high inclination for a particular objective that is not currently a priority of the institution, or high inclination for a gift in the long term but not in the short term. They may have high inclination to support the institution with annual gifts but low inclination to make major gifts. And the larger the gift, in terms of a percentage of the donor's wealth, the more likely that the timing will depend on the donor's personal circumstances more than institutional timelines such as fiscal years or campaign deadlines. Most significantly, inclination usually fails to take into account *philanthropic priority.*

A donor with $100 million in net worth and high inclination will likely be rated $5 million during the planning for a major campaign. When the donor makes a gift of $50,000, the institution might assume that the donor was not inspired by the campaign objectives, didn't relate to institutional leadership, or wasn't properly cultivated or solicited. In many cases, however, the explanation is simpler: The institution is not a high priority in the gift planning of the donor and the donor's family, relative to other institutions. The donor's family may, in fact, be highly impressed by the institution's leaders and vision but have four other institutions they consider to be more important in their philanthropy.

Wealth and inclination do not necessarily translate into priority. Wealthy people, especially those known to be philanthropic, are presented—some would say assaulted—with giving opportunities. They may have high ability and inclination to support dozens of institutions, but rarely will more than a few institutions receive gifts that represent a substantial percentage of their assets. Generous philanthropists will often have a reason to make a one-time gift, and organizations need to understand, despite the size of the gift, that a major gift does not always indicate priority. "It is truly annoying when I tell an organization that a gift is a one-shot deal and they don't hear me," says one leading donor, who has given as much as $100,000 for special purposes without any intention of making the recipient organization a priority in future giving.

Furthermore, more than 90 percent of philanthropists interviewed for this book stated that they have reduced—in most cases, dramatically reduced—the number of organizations they support on a regular basis. Even with their annual gifts, which sometimes run into the six figures, they are cutting back, not on dollars, but on recipients. "I felt like everything was getting diluted," said one donor. "Maybe some of us say 'yes' because it's a friend who is asking, and we think to ourselves, 'I'll do it just this one time.' But it's then hard to say 'no' to others, and all of a sudden, you've made ten gifts of $25,000. [But] $250,000 to just about any one organization can make a huge, if not transformational difference. And that focus allows me to have much greater impact."

Philanthropic priority is also an important factor in the nominating process for new board members. Top programs increasingly require board members to make the institution their top philanthropic priority, or at least to place the institution among their top three priorities, during their term on the board.

As donors prioritize their giving, they also scale their giving. A couple with $100 million, high inclination and a $5 million capacity rating may consider the local animal shelter to be their highest philanthropic priority. In a $5 million shelter campaign, however, even with capacity, inclination and high priority, they are unlikely to make a gift of the full amount of the campaign. They will study the prospective donor list for the campaign, expect that others will do their share and then assess what is needed from them to make the campaign successful. The couple might well determine that a gift of $1 million would be the right scale of gift. Institutions also inadvertently lower sights: If the largest giving opportunity listed in the animal shelter's campaign brochure is $500,000, the same donors might give $500,000 instead of $1 million.

"Fundraisers come to understand that most donors focus on a handful of organizations at most," says Jason Franklin. "If a 'big gift' for your organization is not a 'big gift' for certain donors—in other words, if your organization is not capable of partnering with them at a level they consider to be 'big'—you may not turn out to be among their priorities." To achieve the largest gifts required, then, staff members and volunteers must be able to position the organization for partnership at the highest levels possible, given their vision and strategic plans.

Donors are generally reluctant to share information about their personal wealth. Questions about philanthropic priority, however, are likely to produce informative and even enthusiastic responses. Asking donors to talk about the priorities in their giving and gift planning, and what they most want to accomplish with their philanthropy, accomplishes several things:

- It lets them know you consider them to be giving and generous people.
- It gives you information on how they make giving decisions.
- You learn about other institutions that rank highly in their philanthropic planning, and why.
- It teaches you where they currently rate your institution in their overall philanthropic thinking.

Furthermore, information received directly from donors is almost always more accurate and more persuasive to colleagues when planning cultivation and solicitation activities.

Giving capacity ratings are essential. They help development programs prioritize the deployment of resources, especially human resources, in the cultivation and solicitation of prospective donors. But they are not enough. They must be adjusted to take into account the fact that donors scale their giving. And programs in which wealth capacity is given too much weight waste considerable resources chasing people who are not and never will be philanthropic.

Inclination ratings are also important, but they are rarely useful without detail and context—inclination to give what type of gift, what size of gift, in what timeframe and in what relation to the donor's other giving.

Priority is easier to measure than inclination and, combined with giving capacity, is likely to produce more accurate annual giving and campaign planning projections. Donors who have given your institution high priority should themselves receive high priority attention, and they are among the most important sources of information about how to raise your institution's priority level among other donors. If you don't know your level of priority in a donor's philanthropy, ask the donor!

Finally, asking donors about how and why their priorities for giving have changed over time contributes to your and your institution's understanding of how to move your institution into a place of higher priority.

Chapter 23

ASK DONORS ABOUT THEIR PHILANTHROPIC OBJECTIVES

"The majority of high net worth donors (73 percent) have a specific strategy in place to guide their charitable giving," according to *The 2014 U.S. Trust Study of High Net Worth Philanthropy* (U.S. Trust and Lilly Family School of Philanthropy, 2014). "And a full 93 percent of wealthy donors focus their philanthropic efforts on a targeted set of causes or geographical areas. Only seven percent give with no particular focus."

Philanthropic partnership requires that organizational representatives know the philanthropic objectives of donors and that donors know the objectives of organizations. Organizations are generally good at communicating about their objectives. They publish strategic plans, write press releases announcing new initiatives, produce newsletters, write campaign case statements, and produce fancy brochures and other solicitation pieces, sometimes with elaborate web and video components, outlining exciting giving opportunities. And they send gift officers to spread the word far and wide.

How does the organization learn about the philanthropic objectives of donors? In some cases, donors are clear about their objectives, through their giving and through what they say about their giving. When they have been clear, they expect development officers and other organizational leaders to have done their homework. "I want them to be prepared and to respect the time I'm giving them," says Sandra Rotman. "And I want them to connect their aspirations with what they know about mine."

In many cases, information on philanthropic objectives of individuals and families may be difficult to ascertain. If donors have made only a few gifts, or if they have not said much in the media about their motivations for their past gifts, available research may provide little more than a glimpse into a donor's objectives.

In such cases, the only answer—an obvious answer—is to ask donors what they want to accomplish with their philanthropy *and not just for your organization!* Yet over and over, philanthropists report that they have rarely been asked this simple and straightforward question.

Failing to ask the question says one of two things to a philanthropist: Either the visitor doesn't care about anything other than what the organization needs, or the visitor doesn't believe the donor has philanthropic objectives and is instead just waiting for the right visitor to charm him or her with the best idea ever conceived.

News flash: Philanthropists, especially those who have supported multiple institutions over multiple years, have heard hundreds of "best ideas ever conceived."

The question is not just obvious, when looking through a lens of philanthropic partnership, but it is also easy. Nonphilanthropic people may not be comfortable talking about their philanthropy, but the vast majority of philanthropic people are happy to talk about it and pleased when people show an interest in what they've accomplished and are aiming to accomplish. So the visitor's greatest risk is in finding out that someone is not particularly philanthropic (and maybe making that person wonder why he or she doesn't have a good answer), or in flattering a philanthropist who hasn't yet thought deeply about philanthropy and whose answer might not be well developed. More likely the visitor will be sitting with someone among the 73 percent of donors with philanthropic strategies in place, or at least among the 93 percent who have a focus for their philanthropy and can share, even if they haven't thought a lot about it, what that focus is or has been.

"When someone makes their first gift, a staff member or volunteer needs to ask them why they made it, and ask them what in the organization most captured their interest," says Ann Ziff. "With that information, one is able to do a much better job cultivating their continued interest and involvement. Start with what they want to know, and introduce opportunities for them to learn a little bit more."

Rarely will philanthropic people dodge questions about giving if they view the person asking the questions as someone interested in facilitating their philanthropic objectives, rather than someone merely interested in getting the largest gift possible from them for a specific organization. "You give something of yourself—show who you are and what you care about—and at the same time show that you want to know who the donors are and what they care about," says Robert Zimmer, president of the University of Chicago, who has built partnerships with dozens of transformational gift donors. "Beyond being essential, I find this genuine exchange intrinsically enjoyable."

Philanthropic objectives will not always align immediately. After hearing from donors, organizational representatives are in a much better position to consider how objectives might align and to educate donors who may well be open to expanding their objectives.

Asking about donor objectives and listening carefully to answers, representatives must also be honest when their organizations are not the right partners in accomplishing specific objectives. Representatives who have this courage, and whose organizations will back them up in this honesty, will earn trust from philanthropists. They will find an open door next month, or next year, when changed objectives on the part of philanthropist or organization create the possibility of a successful and mutually rewarding partnership.

Chapter 24

ASK DONORS HOW TO ASK THEM, THANK THEM AND RECOGNIZE THEM

Donors will also tell fundraisers how to ask them for gifts. Take time to learn how families make their philanthropic decisions. Some spouses make independent decisions, some make joint decisions, some make decisions with their children, some involve advisers and some employ all of the above approaches. Most veteran fundraisers have experienced a misstep, working with a donor in one way and learning later that this approach offended a key participant in the decision-making process. The easiest way to avoid such missteps is to ask donors how to ask them, and to keep this dialogue sufficiently open to incorporate changes.

Donors will also describe the ways they prefer to be thanked and recognized, if fundraisers take the time to ask. Here again, preferences vary widely, and missteps put future gifts at risk. "We hate getting plaques, presents and photos," says Jessica Fullerton. "When organizations keep sending stuff, it makes me want to stop giving." "It is likely our name will never be on a building," adds John Fullerton. "But when Ken Burns said he wanted to recognize us by including our names in his films, and when we realized that generations of our descendants would experience this communication from us, and see the work we valued, we found it very appealing."

When putting a name on a building, make sure to balance the organization's preferences for recognition—that might include an unintentionally selfish desire to promote the idea of naming gifts—with a donor's preferences for recognition. Two philanthropists told me they were unhappy with the size of the lettering used to place their names on buildings, in both cases because the lettering was too large. They were not expressing false modesty; they were truly embarrassed.

The number of ways people like to be thanked and recognized is almost as large as the number of major and transformational donors. Each person's preferences are a little different from the next. Why not thank and recognize people the way they want to be thanked?

"For me, it's all about the people," says philanthropist Barbara Lee. "I especially love meeting the young artists we support, buying their work, even helping them price their work, giving them advice on how to get their work out there, and seeing their excitement when their piece gets hung in our collection next to a well-established artist. The best way to thank me is to let me see the impact we are having on their lives. And their expressions of gratitude are so touching; some I'll never forget. For example, as we've helped emerging artists sell their first works, one said to me, 'I made enough money selling my art that I can start a college fund for my kids.' And another, 'Now I can afford to go to the dentist!'"

Experienced fundraisers know that past donors are much more likely to give than nondonors. Recognition done well, therefore, lays the foundation for future gifts. And well-crafted stewardship reports and events inevitably produce new gifts, sometimes right on the spot.

It is not possible to tailor recognition to each and every donor, though as much as can be done should be done. But it surely can and must be done for donors with major and transformational gift capacity.

Finally, pay attention to details. Organizations lose donors every day by misspelling a donor's or spouse's name; by failing to include a spouse in a printed salutation, in a meeting or in an event; or by failing to recognize members of a family individually when that is the family's preference. Donors forgive innocent mistakes, but repeated mistakes lose their innocence, and donor confidence and interest drop.

Chapter 25

GET DONORS INVOLVED

Many organizations have moved away from broad engagement of volunteers in fundraising, in favor of staff-driven activity that is deemed faster and more cost-effective. It is a mistake to expect volunteers to replace staff and save an organization money on fundraising expense. Engaging volunteers, in fact, usually means *more* investment in staff, in order to give volunteers the support they need to make effective contributions to fundraising efforts.

Yet volunteers can do something few staff members can do. They lead by example. They are not paid for their work, so they engage others as peers. Their voluntary contributions are votes of confidence in the organization, its leaders and its plans.

Donors are essential partners in fundraising efforts with other donors. "When staff members are the only voices involved in asking, it is a sign of an impoverished development program," says Dave Dunlop. "Donors add the voice of those who have done themselves what others are being asked to do, at whatever exemplary level that might be. Involving them not only increases the effectiveness of requests, it also recognizes their uniqueness as members of a very special group of organizational friends."

Perhaps most important, they reinforce their own belief and commitment through volunteering. They become better educated about mission, vision and plans. "When we're involved, we will often make a major commitment fairly quickly," says Ann Friedman. "That commitment goes hand in hand with involvement, however; it rarely happens before we're truly involved. And the involvement has to be substantive—we need to feel that our opinions are heard and considered." As volunteers talk with others, they develop an identity as an ambassador of the organization—a stakeholder. As they talk with other donors about gifts, they talk themselves into giving more.

When it comes to those in a position to make major and transformational gifts, "volunteerism is strongly correlated with higher giving levels, and increasingly so," according to *The 2014 U.S. Trust Study of High Net Worth Philanthropy* (U.S. Trust and Lilly Family School of Philanthropy, 2014). "Wealthy donors who volunteered in 2013 gave 73 percent more on average than those who did not volunteer." The study found that 75 percent of wealthy donors volunteer and that "59 percent volunteered more than 100 hours, while 34 percent spent more than 200 hours doing volunteer work. Forty-two percent gave their time to three or more organizations."

Regardless of the type and level of involvement, giving priority is usually tied to degree of involvement, and it pays for organizations to shape meaningful opportunities for involvement as customized as possible to the desires of major and transformational donors and prospective donors. "Levels of involvement vary considerably, but transformational gifts go to the organizations in which donors are the most involved," says Jason Franklin. "When people are on several boards, their transformational gifts will probably go to the organizations connected to their boards. But if donors devote very little time to volunteer service, and if their greatest level of involvement is to serve, for example, as the chair of a gala, chances are that their transformational gifts will include the organization whose gala they chaired."

BOARD SERVICE

Serving as a board member is highly correlated with major and transformational giving. More than 75 percent of the largest and most transformational gifts described by philanthropists interviewed for this book were made to organizations for which a family member was serving or had served on the board. Many philanthropists interviewed have made their largest and most transformational gifts *only* in connection with board service.

"Matthew and I made the largest gift of our lives, at the time, to the music festival and school we had come to love over 50 years," says Kay Bucksbaum, describing their $25 million gift that launched the campaign to renovate the Aspen Music Festival and School's teaching campus, now named in honor of the Bucksbaums. "At different times we each served as board chair, and our leadership roles contributed both to our satisfaction and joy in making this gift and to our understanding of the tremendous impact our gift would have on maintaining the preeminence of the school."

Board membership, however, is not for everyone. "Involve people in ways they want to be involved," says Chris Denby. "Don't always assume board membership is right for them or the organization. Sometimes, putting someone on a board can weaken interest, particularly if that person seeks more active involvement than board membership offers." Many donors interviewed agreed, and most had a story of a board experience that weakened their confidence in an organization. Consider the following examples:

- A person was asked to be on a board, and when she said she didn't have time right now to give proper attention to board duties, she was told she didn't really need to attend board meetings or do any committee work; this indicated to the invitee that she was wanted only for her name or for her money. She declined, and she is unlikely to join the board in the future, when she does have time. "Board members have responsibility for an organization, and I didn't want to read about myself in connection with some governance problem that arose when I wasn't paying attention."

- A person joined a board and learned that all major decisions were made by the board's executive committee. She wasn't on it, so she had little input into key decisions. The rest of the board was expected to rubber-stamp the decisions of the president and executive committee. She resigned.

- Individuals who dominate discussion inhibit the participation of other board members who are not as aggressive. When a board chair doesn't or can't control domineering or overly talkative members, others quietly slip away.

- For the most part, board members don't want to be asked for their name only. If they are invited, they want to know that the organization has thought through the specific contributions needed *beyond* financial contributions. These might include, for example, access to people of influence or expertise developed through professional or civic experience.

By contrast, engaging board members in the right ways strengthens ownership and commitment.

- "One of the best boards on which I've served is the board of Third Way," says Georgette Bennett. "Board meetings never involve a dog and pony show. The board is engaged in the process of thinking through the issues in which Third Way is involved. When organizations give board members an opportunity to get beyond the headlines of an annual report, to see what's really happening, and to make substantive contributions that affect an organization's circumstances and impact, it's tremendously satisfying."
- "At the Whitney Museum of American Art, I'm extremely active, on many committees," says philanthropist Jon Lee. "My colleagues and I feel unbelievably connected to the director, to the entire staff, and to so many others involved with the museum, including fellow board members. It's like a family, so giving is a big pleasure."

Major philanthropists are invited to join more boards than they can possibly handle. Most philanthropists interviewed held their board memberships to between two and six, and most also reported that they were working hard to reduce that number. "I will not agree to join a board without going off another board," was a common refrain. Another common sentiment was, "I don't need another credential. I won't join a board unless I have the time to fulfill the duties that every board member ought to take seriously." "I'm not in the business of lending my nameplate," says philanthropist Joseph Neubauer. "Unless leaders seek my viewpoints in between board meetings, I have no interest in a board seat. I don't need show and tell. I'm happy to help without being a board member, and maybe even contribute. But serving on a board is about getting something done."

OTHER OPPORTUNITIES FOR INVOLVEMENT

Creative leaders find other ways to give philanthropists deep levels of engagement. "There is one organization I support at a major level without serving on the board," says Charles Wall. "I work closely enough with them that I know what's going on. Twice a year I visit campus and meet with the dean and the professor who holds the chair I endowed. They regularly send financial reports showing how my gift is being used. It is important to me to track the impact of my gifts, and their reports make that easy. With this level of access, engagement and knowledge, board membership isn't necessary."

Any involvement should respect the donor's investment of time. Donors should not be asked to give their time without a clear understanding of why that time is needed. Meetings that could have been replaced with a written report are a waste of everyone's time. Yet most philanthropists interviewed talked about meetings—sometimes whole years of service on committees—where they hardly said a word.

Sometimes a short-term engagement—on a task force, or engaging a volunteer in one discussion, or asking one favor, for example—can be more productive and more memorable for all concerned than service on a committee. Knowing they have contributed one essential piece of advice, opened one important door or provided just the right venue for an event can make a volunteer feel much more valuable than sitting through hours of committee meetings.

One example of a fixed-term assignment is a search committee. Numerous philanthropists reported significantly deepening their engagement through service on the search committee for a president or other senior leader such as a music director. At one organization, a top prospective donor had disliked and had been quietly though highly critical of a president, wanting little engagement. When that president left, the board asked this philanthropist to serve on the presidential search committee, and a relationship that formed through the search blossomed into a strong commitment to the new president. The relationship resulted in one of the largest gifts the organization had ever received.

Chapter 26

WITH BOARDS, FOCUS ON COLLECTIVE RESPONSIBILITY

Board members are among the most important and engaged philanthropic partners, in most organizations. They also play a key role in strengthening partnerships within the board and across the organization's wider major and transformational donor population.

Requirements for personal giving of board members vary widely by organization and by type of board. Boards of most nonprofits set an annual expectation of 100 percent participation in giving. Most financially stable or strong nonprofits also rely on board members to provide a significant percentage of overall gift dollars in annual campaigns and in capital campaigns. Other potential donors regularly ask presidents and development directors about the commitment of board members to fundraising efforts.

There is no one-size-fits-all formula for board support. Organizations with board members giving $500 per year thrive while other organizations with board members giving $50,000 per year struggle. Organizations with a broad donor base and 10 percent of total funding coming from board members succeed while others whose board members provide 75 percent of total revenue struggle.

With few exceptions, the boards of successful organizations adopt clear expectations related to the collective responsibilities of the board, and they evaluate prospective and current board members within this larger framework.

COLLECTIVE RESPONSIBILITY
FOR PHILANTHROPIC SUPPORT

Whether the need for private support is measured in the thousands or in the hundreds of millions, the most successful organizations have boards with a shared understanding, across their membership, of collective responsibility for philanthropic support in the context of overall collective responsibility to the organization. That shared understanding informs annual and long-term planning, goal setting and budgeting, giving plans for each board member, and the recruitment of new board members.

By contrast, organizations without a shared understanding and commitment to collective responsibility among board members usually experience unproductive tension and frustration among board members and between board members and administrators. Too often board members are recruited without a clear picture of what is expected of the board as a whole and of them specifically. Rarely does the recruitment involve a detailed discussion of where the organization will fit in the overall philanthropic plans and priorities of the people being recruited. As a result, when new board members are eventually presented with a gift proposal, they rarely understand how the proposed gift fits into the larger picture of what is expected of them and their fellow board members. A gift they believe to be generous may turn out to be a great disappointment to the organization, creating financial challenges that in turn lead to finger-pointing, blame, embarrassment and kneejerk solutions.

Finger-pointing includes grumbling among CEOs and development officers, and sometimes board members themselves, about board members who aren't giving "enough." Without a clear understanding of the board's collective responsibility and the part that each member plays, some board members inevitably come to feel that they are carrying too much of the weight, while others feel that their generous contributions aren't appreciated. Finger-pointing also includes complaints among board members about administrators who aren't developing sufficiently strong relationships with board members, aren't attracting new donors, and aren't creating compelling gift opportunities. There is always more than enough blame to go around!

Kneejerk solutions include establishing or enforcing term limits to remove board members. Term limits may help remove individuals who are not giving at required levels, but they may also lead to the loss of individuals who have been among the organization's most generous benefactors. Furthermore, individuals removed may resent the implication that their gifts of time, talent and treasure were insufficient, especially when giving expectations changed after they were recruited or were never articulated in the first place.

Sudden or substantial changes in minimum giving expectations can sometimes be an unproductive, arbitrary solution. New minimum expectations, applied across a group of people who were not recruited with the same expectations in place, almost always offend those without the capacity to meet them while *lowering* the sights of individuals with much greater capacity. They can also upset the balance of financial and other considerations when assessing the overall contributions required of the board.

Much more productive is an approach that allows the board to define its members' collective responsibility to the organization, in the context of the organization's needs and aspirations, the size and wealth of the organization's prospective donor base, and the organization's competitive landscape. Defining responsibility in this way prevents the conversation from becoming inappropriately personal. It also allows for more realistic strategic planning and more comprehensive and sustainable board development. The board chair, board members, the CEO and the chief development officer are all essential participants in this process; it cannot be accomplished without active involvement of the board and commitment of board leaders. Once collective responsibility is defined and understood, changes in aspiration that are embraced by the board lead naturally to changes in collective responsibility. Board members make decisions about planning *and* their overall responsibility as a board at the same time; these are no longer disconnected considerations.

ASSESSING COLLECTIVE RESPONSIBILITY

Board chairs, CEOs and chief development officers often ask how much any given board should be giving. The answer is that boards, except in special cases, must provide *leadership* in their collective personal financial commitments and in their commitments to help their organizations raise funds from others. But "leadership" varies from organization to organization. Successful campaigns might involve boards giving a total of 10 percent of campaign dollars while others involve boards that provide 90 percent of total support. Administrative and board leaders assist boards in assessing collective philanthropic responsibility by examining the following:

- The organization's needs and aspirations, and the degree and rate of growth required

- The size of the board and the sizes of boards of peer organizations
- The total percentage of private support provided by boards of peer organizations in the community, regionally and nationally, as applicable
- The average annual gift required of board members to meet current and projected needs, and an assessment of how this would change according to the size of the board
- The size and collective capacity of the current donor base and of the prospective donor base, beyond board members
- The nonfinancial contributions required of board members for success in fulfilling mission and meeting strategic objectives

All of these factors should be considered when assessing collective responsibility and collective capacity of the board. Adding or changing term limits may be wise but only when done in concert with other changes that collectively improve overall board capacity. Adding or raising a minimum giving expectation may be highly effective but only when designed in a way that raises the sights of all concerned. Some boards, for example, have found great success in establishing board dues that ensure a basic level of unrestricted support without diminishing the organization's ability to engage in gift discussions above and beyond the dues. The key in all these decisions is to consider and apply each in the context of a larger understanding of collective responsibility.

EXAMPLES

In one small organization, the total revenue from giving was approximately $125,000. The organization was running a structural deficit of approximately $30,000. There was no minimum expectation of board members; most board members gave $250 or less, and board giving totaled $9,000. Giving was never discussed during the recruitment of new board members. A benchmarking study of six peer organizations showed board giving that ranged from $2,000 to $5,000 per year per board member. The board collectively adopted an expectation that existing and new board members would be asked to give a minimum of $1,000 and collectively increase board giving from 7 percent of total giving to 14 percent of total giving. One of the organization's nonboard donors, upon learning of the board's renewed commitment, pledged $10,000 per year. The structural deficit was erased.

In another organization, prior to contemplating a $75 million campaign, the nominating committee had been recommending new board members strictly based on a history of annual giving. Those with annual giving of $10,000 or more were considered strong candidates. Studying peer organizations, and with a lead gift of $25 million for the new campaign from a board member in hand, the board and administration determined that the board's collective responsibility to the campaign would need to be $25 million in addition to the lead gift—in other words, one-third of total campaign dollars would come from the lead donor, one-third from the rest of the board, and the remaining one-third from all other donors. The nominating process took that into account; new board members now have the capacity and inclination to give $500,000, on average. For each board member with less capacity, the committee looks for another with more capacity, so that the average capability of the board will allow the board, collectively, to play the leadership role required. Board gifts to the campaign, since the lead gift, have ranged from $25,000 to $5 million, but the board's part of the campaign is more than 95 percent complete.

Another organization, contemplating a $4 to $5 billion campaign, studied peer organizations and determined that the board's collective responsibility would need to be $1 billion, or 20 to 25 percent of the new campaign. This would require board member giving to average more than $10 million. Rather than state that each board member was expected to give $10 million, the organization factored this collective responsibility into the nominating process. Some board members, recognizing the need for greater giving capacity of the board as a whole, elected to step off the board at the end of their terms and get involved in other ways. Others stayed on, given their other important contributions beyond financial support. And the nominating committee sought candidates who, on average, could raise the collective capability. Prospective board members with $100 million giving capacity knew they would not be carrying the full weight themselves, and prospective board members with $1 million giving capacity knew that they would need to stretch and make the organization their highest philanthropic priority for the period of the campaign. *Collectively,* the board repositioned itself to support the strategic plans they themselves had adopted for the organization.

SUMMARY

Regardless of scale of need, every organization will benefit from a thoughtful, inclusive consideration of the board's collective leadership responsibility in the context of the organization's vision and ambition. Instilling a sense of ownership in the organization's planning greatly increases the potential for philanthropic engagement of a board member, as for any donor. Ownership felt in the context of collective responsibility of the board further increases the likelihood that the board member will make a gift that colleagues on the board will see as an appropriate stretch, and to which colleagues will respond with similar generosity and satisfaction.

Requirements in time, talent and treasure, and the balance among these, vary by organization. Organizations that require tremendous investments of time may decide that, collectively, they need some board members who give several hours every week, even with limited financial capacity; other board members who write large checks but have little discretionary time; and many others in between. It is the collective contribution that matters, in terms of the organization's ultimate success.

In all organizations, even those that require billions of dollars of financial support, giving capacity will vary by board member. Collective philanthropic responsibility will make it unlikely that a board requiring $1 billion in board giving will decide to recruit a board member who can give only $1,000 per year. But a shared understanding of collective responsibility will lead to an appropriate range being set; more transparency and better understanding among all board members of the contributions of others; greater confidence among board members in the importance and impact of their individual contributions; and a greater likelihood that *all* board members will share in the feeling of accomplishment when the campaign is finished, the buildings are built, and the needs of society are served, and will say, together, "We did this."

Chapter 27

INTRODUCE DONORS TO COLLEAGUES

The work of a fundraising staff member or volunteer focused on major and transformational giving is first and foremost to build relationships that lead to philanthropic partnership. Leading philanthropists report multiple relationships with people involved in the organizations they support—presidents, staff members, board members, other donors and so on. The higher the priority in their giving, in general, the more relationships they have.

Beyond strengthening donor confidence in leadership, vision, planning and financial responsibility, relationships throughout an organization feed the very passion that drives giving. "My support of the arts has allowed me to meet amazing people who enrich my life," says Mercedes Bass. "I learn a lot from them, and it's great fun to be with them. They include world-renowned soloists but also the people who build an organization's artistic reputation each and every day—the conductor, the orchestra players, the chorus master, the chorus members and so on. Right after my first major gift to the Metropolitan Opera, general manager Joe Volpe took me on stage as soon as the curtain came down and introduced me to the whole chorus. It's a moment I'll never forget."

Bruce Clinton agrees. "Sitting in a finance committee meeting, going over the agenda, I noticed that the Chicago Symphony Orchestra was hoping to purchase new timpani," he says. "I had at one point in my life considered becoming a professional timpanist. I began thinking about it in the meeting, and over the next few days the romance of the idea caught me. We made the gift, and that set a whole process in motion. We were introduced to the new timpanist, got to know him, and then he and his family came and visited us in Colorado for a few days. A nice relationship developed. Not long after, the symphony approached me and asked if we'd consider naming a chair in timpani. We're not big on naming anything, but once again, the flirtation with timpani kicked in, and we did it. The next time we were in Chicago, we went to a performance, and when we went backstage, the timpanist insisted we join him on stage for a photo. We've had nothing but genuine emotional delight in the whole experience, and we have a new and wonderful friend."

Fundraisers—whether presidents, program leaders or development officers—who meet with donors and fail to introduce others into the relationship do a great disservice to their organizations and to donors as well. Every seasoned gift officer has encountered a donor—if not dozens—who have experienced hiatuses of engagement ranging from months to years. "You're the third gift officer I've seen in ten years, and I haven't seen anyone for the past five years" is not an uncommon refrain. While gift officer turnover is noticed, it is much less consequential when the gift officer is one of several contact points between donor and organization.

Fostering relationships with multiple leaders within the same organization greatly reduces the risk of loss of confidence when a president or other senior leader leaves the organization. The best principal gift programs support relationships between leading donors and a variety of other leaders including other donors, board members, administrative leaders and programmatic leaders.

Performance measurements and bonus structures can inadvertently lead to siloed relationship building, especially when fundraisers, even presidents, believe they will get more credit when they are seen as being principally responsible for specific gifts. Such belief, and the behavior that follows, ultimately weakens philanthropic partnership and long-term fundraising potential. Wise leaders find ways to incentivize teamwork and collaboration.

Though they require more creativity and more discussion between manager and gift officer, metrics tied to depth and quality of donor engagement are much more important, in major and transformational giving programs, than metrics tied simply to gift officer activity such as number of visits or number of proposals written. Measuring and valuing donor engagement inevitably encourages expansion of relationships between donor and organization.

Introducing donors to colleagues also improves organization-wide understanding of donor objectives and minimizes misunderstanding or conflict. Knowledge of donor objectives among all relevant leaders reduces the potential for internal jealousy or strife among those whose programs don't benefit from that donor's gift, strife that has great potential to harm philanthropic partnership, especially if donors become aware of it.

For example, a chief development officer once worked with two deans who had done a wonderful job, separately, of cultivating a very generous couple. The couple had degrees from both schools. The deans had a great relationship with each other, but they each privately made clear to the development officer that the couple could only be asked for one gift, and "it had better not be for that other dean's school."

Rather than ignoring one dean, or trying to negotiate with both deans—perhaps working out a "deal" that might make no sense at all to the donors—the development officer suggested the deans meet with the donors together. The result was a joint gift. The donors remarked that they were so pleased to see how collaborative the two deans were and that this added tremendously to their *confidence* in making the gift. Equally important, the creative solution proposed by the chief development officer resulted in strengthened relationships when the conflict could easily have damaged them.

When dealing with complex issues that involve multiple parts of an organization, or even multiple organizations, many philanthropists enjoy getting to know all the key players. "People who choose to work on the big challenges facing society are usually driven by a deep passion," says Ann Doerr. "And they're smart. I love being around smart people who share my passion. It feeds me intellectually and increases my desire to be involved."

Chapter 28

INTRODUCE DONORS TO EACH OTHER— LET THEM SPREAD BELIEF AND CONFIDENCE

At the University of Chicago, as part of launching our principal gift program, we invited the 50 families with the highest cumulative giving to a reception. The board chair and his wife opened their home for the occasion. We were thrilled with the response—over 90 percent attended, some traveling from great distances. What we had not appreciated before the event was how few of these families had ever met. We knew their names by heart. But they didn't know each other. The simple act of introducing them to each other, and letting them talk with each other, perceptibly reinforced their individual decisions to make the university a priority in their giving.

The enlightened president of an opera company, upon meeting the new head of a local school of music, immediately invited the educational leader to a gathering of opera donors. "If they enjoy giving to support your music students, they'll be even more excited about giving to the opera," he said. Some board members and development officers might react in horror, hearing their president speak this way. But the opera president was right, and the two leaders continually reinforced donor confidence in both organizations by introducing arts patrons to others who shared their passion.

This mutual confidence building among donors can cross geographical as well as organizational lines. "A friend, who runs a major art museum, had the idea that involving some of his donors with prominent donors in the world of art beyond his museum would be beneficial to his fundraising," says one donor. "I enjoy meeting other arts donors, and we do indeed encourage each other's philanthropy. I was thrilled to see that one of the couples I had met on several occasions recently made an eight-figure gift to that museum."

Donors, generally speaking, prefer to be in the company of others. Through matching programs, challenge gifts, or simply through effective communication about a gift, they invite others to join them. "A gift can be much more powerful than its dollar value alone," says Chris Denby. "It can be crafted to have a multiplier effect. I structure every gift I make in a way that inspires other donors or enhances an organization's ability to bring other donors on board."

Friendships—sometimes deep and lifelong friendships—spring from engagement among donors. And these friendships in turn strengthen the connection between the donors and the organizations they support, and their sense of pleasure and pride of association. "The most important part of any organization is the people," say philanthropists Bob and Nancy Magoon. "Great things happen when a group of people work together and pull in the same direction. We've made so many wonderful friends through our involvement as donors and board members. Creating a sense of family deepens everyone's commitment and adds immeasurably to our satisfaction in giving."

Chapter 29

PRACTICE PHILANTHROPIC PARTNERSHIP

Beyond asking donors about their philanthropic motivations and objectives, and beyond reading about and observing successful partnerships, another way to learn is to practice partnership. Practice might include serving on a nonprofit board or making a partnership gift. Breaking down silos to partner internally also improves partnership-building skills.

SERVE ON A BOARD

Board members sit simultaneously on both sides of the partnership table. They are typically among an organization's principal donors, and at the same time their work as board members has an impact on many aspects of donor, leader, staff member, and volunteer belief and confidence:

- They hire and fire the CEO, who in turn appoints and supervises other organizational leaders.
- They contribute to strategic planning.
- They oversee financial planning and preserve long-term financial health and stability.
- They inject early confidence in plans and in fundraising efforts through leadership gifts.

Serving on a board enhances understanding, from a variety of angles, about how to build and sustain effective philanthropic partnerships.

MAKE A PARTNERSHIP GIFT

One of the best ways to learn about donor perspectives on philanthropic partnership is to be a partnership donor and learn directly from one's own experience. Think carefully about your own philanthropic objectives, then find an organization whose mission, vision and plans align with your objectives. Make a gift that allows the organization to accomplish something they might not have been able to accomplish without you, and that allows you to do something for society that is meaningful to you. It doesn't take a lot—last year, a highly talented student was accepted to the Aspen Music Festival and School on a full scholarship. The problem: He didn't have $250 for the bus fare across the country. A gift of $250 made all the difference.

PARTNER INTERNALLY
TO PARTNER EXTERNALLY

Partnership begins in the office. Everyone who has ever worked in fundraising knows that internal partnership is one of the first things to suffer in the face of ambitious fundraising goals. Competition can be healthy, but it can easily cross the line and weaken productivity. Fundraisers, including administrative leaders, may think this breakdown in internal partnership is invisible to philanthropists, but they are usually wrong.

Before trying to build partnerships with donors, build strong and healthy partnerships with colleagues. And when those partnerships are threatened, delete the angry email and instead walk to your colleague's office.

In building a partnership, whether with another part of the organization or even between two organizations, you might also find efficiency and increased effectiveness in the collaboration. Such collaboration is appealing to knowledgeable donors, who want their gift dollar to go further. Numerous philanthropists proudly told stories of their own initiatives to drive collaboration, some of which are included in Chapter 18. Those organizations had to be ready, on some level, to partner—otherwise, the donors would have found other organizations that were better prepared.

One of the most important internal partnerships related to fundraising is the partnership between CEO and chief development officer. That partnership is more important than ever, given the fundraising pressures on CEOs and the expectations on chief development officers related to and beyond fundraising (see Schiller, 2013).

Chapter 30

CONSIDER YOUR APPROACH

Pursuing philanthropic partnership, rather than transactional giving, changes not only the language but also the whole mindset and approach of all partners involved—donors and organizational representatives.

USE LANGUAGE THAT SUPPORTS PHILANTHROPIC PARTNERSHIP

The fundraising profession, like other professions, has its own language. Professional terminology has advantages and disadvantages. It facilitates communication among colleagues within and across institutional boundaries. But it also carries potential for misunderstanding and weakening of philanthropic partnership.

Some language distances or dehumanizes donors. "Prospective donor" shortened to "prospect" becomes yet more impersonal. "Suspect," when used to mean someone who might become a "prospect" once more is learned, is another common term better reserved for staff shorthand than for reports in front of board members and other donors. "Moves management," a successful and widely used approach, is regrettably named in the view of Dave Dunlop, an early adopter and promoter of the concept. "We ought not feel, nor suggest through the use of this terminology, that we are 'putting the moves' on our generous friends," says Dave.

Terms applied to those who work with donors can also strengthen or weaken a culture of partnership. "Prospect manager" may be understood by the holder of the title, or by others, to convey an unhealthy degree of control over access to the prospective donor being "managed." Some prospect managers see themselves as gatekeeper or even owner of a relationship, whereas more experienced and successful prospect managers think of themselves as "facilitators" and "liaisons."

Every strategy session, cultivation plan, solicitation discussion and stewardship report offers an opportunity to reinforce the language of partnership.

Need versus shared objective

Guided by an organization's mission, leaders create strategic objectives that respond to current opportunities. Strategic objectives drive operational planning, and resulting plans require funding.

Mission is also, usually, at the heart of donor affiliation. Committed to the same mission, some, if not many, existing donors are predisposed to develop a shared sense of the importance and urgency of objectives designed to extend an organization's impact on society.

If an organization waits until the focus has shifted to need, the opportunity to create a sense of shared objective is greatly diminished, unless the shared objective already exists. Involving prospective donors at an earlier stage in the process, therefore, increases the chance of developing a shared sense of ownership. It also opens an organization to the possibility that a donor, who shares a commitment to mission, will bring additional experience and perspective to the planning process that results in a stronger outcome.

Placing an emphasis on "need" also distances the donor. An organization's "need" is not the motivating factor for most major and transformational gift donors. Talking about "need" conveys, "I am trying to do something important and the thing stopping me is lack of money." Major and transformational gifts are motivated by shared objective—by opportunity. Donors and facilitators alike say, "If we combine our resources, we'll be able to do something important."

Evaluate every appeal. Does it portray a successful organization with the capacity to do more, in partnership with generous friends, or does it portray an organization desperate to balance the budget, hopeful that it will still be around next year? Needy organizations inspire small gifts, whereas organizations that *meet* needs and demonstrate a clear financial capacity to do so enlist major donor partners. The vast majority of nonprofit organizations need more money to accomplish their objectives, but this does not make them *needy.*

One of the best indicators of success in shifting the focus to shared objectives is the frequency with which donors refer to objectives in the first person, rather than in the third person. Rather than saying, "*They* are finding a cure for cancer," these donors say, "*We* are finding a cure for cancer."

Indebtedness versus mutual benefit

Emphasizing indebtedness is another arms-length approach. When donors talk about "paying a debt," they are rarely discussing what for them is a major or transformational gift, or if it is a major gift, paying a debt is rarely the principal motivating factor. Like ability to impress, indebtedness may create an opening for engagement with a prospective donor. But mutual benefit, like mutual respect, is the ingredient found in successful philanthropic partnerships.

This does not mean *quid pro quo,* as in giving a gift in order to get a child into a private school. Rather, mutual benefit means allowing both philanthropist and organization to get something done that is important to each.

DON'T TRY TO IMPRESS; BUILD MUTUAL RESPECT

Every day, leaders develop plans; flesh out details; and then turn their attention to language, drawings, events, and other vehicles designed to impress prospective donors. Redirecting some or even most of this time and effort into developing mutual respect and into creating shared objectives built on that foundation of respect, successful facilitators of philanthropic partnership find that prospective donors don't need to be impressed. Impressive plans and impressive results may capture the attention of new potential philanthropic partners, but genuine engagement and mutual respect is what will lead to plans in which *they* invest.

Other ways of trying to capture mindshare of donors backfire when they are insincere. "Asking for advice when you don't really want it destroys mutual respect," says Paula Crown, "as does letting people think *this* is where you're headed when your real agenda is to do *that.* Donors come to resent leaders who bait and switch or pretend to ask for input when they really intend to steer to a preordained destination."

"Some institutions convene task forces and committees that take up enormous amounts of time," adds Jeanette Lerman-Neubauer. "They solicit reports with problem-solving recommendations. Then they ignore the conclusions and ask for checks to sustain business as usual. If I had been in agreement, I could have liberated time and just written a check. But if not, the process is quite alienating."

GRATITUDE FIRST ...

Donors rarely complain that they are thanked too often. Sadly, those who give the most, and the most often, find themselves taken for granted. "I don't like when people make a fuss over a gift, but a basic 'thank you' is crucially important," says one leading philanthropist. "The person who understands this best is the leader of one of the smallest organizations I support. But no matter what I do, I get a handwritten note, and sometimes I even get flowers. That organization can count on my support without question."

The appropriate response to a gift is, "Thank you." Sadly, many partnerships fail to materialize or are destroyed when volunteers, organizational leaders, or staff members forget this very simple fact, something we all should have learned as young children. When the desired gift is the newest and hottest gadget and the actual gift is the ugliest sweater ever made, the appropriate response is, "Thank you." When the desired gift is $1 million and the actual gift is $100,000, *the appropriate response is, "Thank you."* The donor didn't have to give $1, let alone $100,000.

A board member of an organization in a campaign, deeply excited about the campaign's objectives, decided with his wife upon a stretch gift, 10 times the size of any gift they had previously given. Their decision was one of the hardest, and one of the happiest, of their lives. Arriving at the next board meeting, the board chair took the donor aside, just before the meeting. The donor was not expecting any special attention, but he was pleased that the board member knew about the gift and was, evidently, going to take a few minutes to thank him in person. "I understand you made a commitment to the campaign," began the board chair, "and while it is generous, I hope you might consider doubling that gift." Stunned, the board member took his seat, all pleasure in the gift erased. "I almost wanted to ask for the gift back, given the number of other organizations we could have helped with that money."

Another donor, who had made multiple seven- and eight-figure gifts, joined a board. Without being asked, the donor sent a multimillion-dollar gift to the president. "In my experience, it's unusual for someone to agree to join a board, agree to a large annual gift, and then, right at the beginning, and unsolicited, make a large capital gift. There was virtually no expression of thanks. All I can think is that the president and board had wanted much more and that they were so disappointed, they didn't know what to do! Needless to say, that was my last major gift to that organization."

... THEN RESULTS

Gratitude goes a long way, but it does not sustain a philanthropic partnership unless it is coupled with results. In fact, saying "thank you" without delivering on the promise of the gift destroys the mutual respect required to sustain a partnership. Results need not be perfect; informed and engaged donors usually stand by organizational leaders as unanticipated obstacles arise. But the donor who has to ask, months or years later, "Whatever happened with my last gift?" enters any new gift conversation, if he or she enters one at all, with diminished confidence.

"We wanted to do something about women's rights, and we were inspired by the plans of one prominent organization working in that space," said one couple who have made multiple seven- and eight-figure gifts. "We sent $100,000 unsolicited. We never heard anything about how the gift was used or the impact of the gift. Naturally, that was our first and last gift."

By contrast, results build confidence, and this increased confidence makes each subsequent gift conversation easier, if not altogether unnecessary. Philanthropists who find a capable partner become more and more likely to initiate conversations about how to expand their impact.

"Without any question, our greatest satisfaction in giving comes from impact—tangible impact on people's lives," says Jim Crown, speaking on behalf of the Crown family, a family that supports hundreds of organizations every year and has made more than a dozen eight-figure gifts. "It's nice to be nice to the nice, but that's a bad way to think about philanthropy. Looking good and feeling good are nice, but doing good, with evidence that what you've done has made a difference, is what's important."

Criteria by which results will be measured should be discussed up front and understood by both donor and organization. The degree of desired detail may vary, but donors want to know, in measurable terms, the difference their gift is expected to make. They also want to have confidence that organizational leaders will regularly evaluate and adjust investments for maximum impact, and that they will receive accurate reports on results. "It puzzles me when business leaders don't apply metrics to their philanthropy," says Joseph Neubauer. "Whether you're leading a for-profit business, serving on the board of a nonprofit organization, or investing philanthropically, you're in the resource allocation business. Measurement of return on investment is essential."

"Organizations and philanthropists need to measure results and deliver on promises," adds Tim Gill. "Philanthropists should and will cut off programs and organizations that don't work and move on to something that does."

KEEP A LONG-TERM VIEW

Institutional structures, ambitious goals, aggressive timelines and other institution-centric factors can lead to behavior that emphasizes quantity of activity with donors, including quantity of solicitations, over quality. Yet giving remains deeply personal. Building relationships that lead to major and transformational giving requires a focus on quality rather than quantity. It also requires willingness—and sufficient time—to develop plans appropriate to each relationship.

Successful facilitators of philanthropic partnership trust their gut when planning and implementing cultivation and solicitation activities. When a proposed gift discussion with a donor doesn't feel right—in tone or timing— they go back to the drawing board. They consistently place a higher value on long-term partnerships than on short-term financial goals.

MEASURE THE RIGHT THINGS

As organizations strive for the best possible return on investments in fund-raising staff and programs, and as the development profession has matured, organizational leaders have understandably placed greater emphasis on measurement. Conference sessions, if not entire fundraising conferences, focus on how to design and implement "metrics."

Quantitative measures, not surprisingly, are easier to develop than quali-tative measures. Effective managers develop and pay attention to qualitative measures, ensuring that transactional behavior supports rather than detracts from philanthropic partnership.

BE AUTHENTIC

Paid and unpaid representatives of an organization can—though they should not!—get away with a degree of inauthenticity in short-term, transactional fundraising. Inauthenticity, however, has no place in philanthropic partnerships. Potential partners expect and deserve honesty and transparency in all aspects of their relationship with the organization and its leaders. They want and need to know the good, the bad, and even—when critical to ensuring a long-term relationship—the ugly. They want to understand risks as well as potential rewards.

Authentic facilitators of philanthropic partnership never suggest that a project is a higher priority than is really the case, simply to secure a gift. They do not sell giving opportunities that are not fully cooked, nor do they promise an outcome that they know is unlikely to be delivered. They plan carefully and build consensus around their plans, allowing them to make promises on which they can deliver.

Most major donors won't bad-mouth an organization that has been dishonest with them; they will simply avoid moving from transactional support to deeper partnerships that lead to major and transformational support. Or they may quietly disappear altogether. "Truth is paramount," says one major philanthropist. "The president of one organization I supported lied in a public statement about a gift, and I quietly called him on it. Not too long after, he told the same lie! He was eventually fired, but I had lost confidence in the organization and never went back."

One couple shared a heartbreaking story: Another couple deeply involved with an organization befriended this couple, and over many months—more than a year—enjoyed dinners, performances and other social meetings, in addition to business meetings, connected with the organization. Upon making a multimillion-dollar commitment, the couple that was new to the organization never heard from the other couple again. They were hurt—they felt they had been developing a long-term friendship, and instead, they were being cultivated for a gift, nothing more, nothing less.

Donors who have found authentic, truthful partners, however, often form lifelong professional—and even personal—bonds. Those bonds are one of the greatest rewards of participation in philanthropic work, for donors and for those privileged to facilitate their work. In effective relationships, partners say what they will do and then do what they say. They keep their promises. They are authentic.

FLEXIBILITY

When donors face challenges in personal circumstances, organizational partners respond with understanding and flexibility. In an economic downturn, focus on short-term commitments, such as outright gifts, rather than multiple-year pledges. Whether a donor has $100,000 or $100 million, if they've suddenly lost 30 percent of their net worth, they may well be concerned that they could lose another 30 percent tomorrow. If pushed to make a five-year commitment, it will likely be a fraction of the amount they truly want to give. An outright one-time gift, or even a short-term pledge, however, can be made with a higher degree of confidence in ability to pay.

When other circumstances reduce assets, whether throughout the economy or specific to an individual donor, respond with flexibility, and keep a long view. Especially for consistent and loyal donors, offer flexibility in payment schedules on existing pledges. And avoid embarrassing those who can't make a donor-society-level annual gift that they've made for dozens of years in a row: Invite them to attend the recognition event anyway.

Such gestures are rarely forgotten and often repaid many times over. When a donor couple lost a substantial portion of their net worth in the Madoff scandal, they had to reduce levels of giving across several institutions they had supported generously for many years. In most, they were dropped unceremoniously from the donor rolls, but in one organization, the president reached out, letting them know they would be listed as donors and invited to all events for as long as they wished. They recovered, after a few years, and that organization has a much higher priority in their giving decisions, now and for many years into the future.

When a spouse dies, it can take years for the surviving spouse to settle into a new economic reality and understand what he or she is able to give. Smart organizations give surviving spouses time and space to recover. Here again, for those who have been loyal supporters, don't drop them just because they are focused on things other than your fiscal year!

Finally, when donors who have given at the highest levels for many years are no longer capable of giving at the same level because they have moved to a fixed income, consider letting them stay in the president's circle as lifetime members, recognizing a lifetime of support. Let the spirit of partnership—of working together to build and sustain great organizations—prevail. Your generosity in recognizing all they have done may keep your organization in their last wills—the ones that matter—when donors look back on their lives and think about the organizations that have been their *partners* in life, not merely recipients of their largesse.

SUMMARY

Words and deeds have the potential to contribute to or detract from a healthy environment for major and transformational gift fundraising. Building and sustaining a culture of philanthropic partnership takes more than the decision of a leader or group of leaders. It requires a series of intentional small decisions in support of such a culture, made throughout an organization, each and every day.

Chapter 31

EVERYONE HAS A
ROLE TO PLAY

Every person involved with a nonprofit organization has the ability to increase overall levels of belief and confidence.

A long-serving nonprofit chief financial officer recently told me that one of the most important things she has learned from her organization's president is that everything she does and says in meetings with board members has the potential to enhance or reduce their confidence in the organization. She believes her organization is a worthy recipient of gifts and an excellent steward. And she has come to understand that it's important to the organization that the manner in which she talks with her staff and the manner in which she presents reports convey that belief. Among other reasons, many of her largest donors are on the finance and investment committees—as is true for many organizations.

Every staff member, volunteer and "customer"—student, patient, audience member, etc.—of an organization has the capacity to build confidence. Their words and their work, therefore, have an impact on fundraising. Contributing to success in fundraising need not involve asking for money, attending fundraising events, or even knowing a donor or anyone on the development staff. Philanthropic partnership depends on pride of affiliation. That pride is contagious, and the more people who have it and show it, the more likely major philanthropists will see it and feel it.

One way every staff member can contribute to belief and confidence is by being a donor, even with a gift of $10. Staff members in nonprofit organizations are usually not wealthy, but they can be philanthropic. When they believe in what their own organization does, a decision to give can have a powerful effect on other donors. One president told me that his organization recently achieved 100 percent staff participation in a campaign. The board and other top donors were overwhelmed and thrilled to learn of this extraordinary vote of confidence.

BE PROUD OF WHAT YOU DO

Those involved in building and sustaining philanthropic partnerships should be proud of what they do. Great organizations throughout the United States and around the globe depend on philanthropic partners. When philanthropy thrives, the world is a better place to live. When leaders, staff members, or volunteers contribute to an environment that enables philanthropy, they can derive tremendous satisfaction, not merely through the achievement of fundraising goals, but through the impact on society that they have enabled.

"I am privileged to work with the better angels of humankind," says fundraising professional Jim Thompson. "What our donors and organizational leaders do literally touches and shapes the ages. What's not to love about that?"

THE FIRST THING YOU CAN DO

The next time a board or staff colleague expresses discomfort with involvement in fundraising, ask that person if he or she believes in and has confidence in the organization. If the answer is "yes," ask why. Then ask that person to tell someone else.

BELIEF AND CONFIDENCE CHECKLIST

This checklist may be used to evaluate the potential for philanthropic partnership between an individual donor and an organization. It may also be used to evaluate the overall readiness of an organization to build and sustain philanthropic partnerships.

In each blank, insert "S" for strong, "A" for average, and "W" for weak.

Potential Donor Has:

___ Belief in the importance of giving

___ Confidence in present and future personal financial circumstances

___ Confidence in overall personal circumstances

___ Belief in the organization's mission

___ Confidence in the organization's leaders

___ Belief in vision and confidence in the organization's strategy

___ Confidence in the organization's financial strength and stability

___ Confidence in the organization's capacity to raise additional funds from others

Organizational Leaders Have:

___ Belief that their organization is worthy of philanthropic investment at the levels they are seeking

___ Belief and confidence in each other's leadership, vision, strategy, and planning

___ Confidence in their chief development officer and their development program

___ Confidence in their organization's capacity to meet fundraising goals

___ Belief in philanthropic partnership

Staff Members and Volunteers Have:

___ Belief in their organization's mission

___ Confidence in their organization's leaders, plans, and goals

___ Belief that their individual contributions make a difference

Ratings of "A" (average) suggest that discussion is needed. Increased awareness may be sufficient to convert these ratings to "S" (strong). Ratings of "W" (weak) will likely require awareness-building, commitment to change, a clear and measurable plan for change, and regular monitoring.

BIBLIOGRAPHY

"A kid from Peabody High School," *Tepper Magazine,* Fall 2004.

O'Clery, Conor. *The Billionaire Who Wasn't.* New York: PublicAffairs, Perseus Books Group, 2007.

Panas, Jerold. *Mega Gifts* (2nd ed.). Medfield, MA: Emerson & Church, 2005.

Schiller, Ronald J. *The Chief Development Officer.* New York: Rowman & Littlefield, 2013.

Seymour, Harold J. *Designs for Fund-Raising.* New York: McGraw-Hill, 1966.

Sider, Alison. "GSB Nets $300 Million Gift from Alumnus David Booth." *Chicago Maroon,* November 7, 2008. *http://chicagomaroon.com/2008/11/07/gsb-nets-300-million-gift-from-alumnus-david-booth/.*

University of Chicago Medicine. "About Gary C. Comer," 2006. *http://www.uchicagokids hospital.org/fact/gary-comer.html.*

U.S. Trust and Lilly Family School of Philanthropy. *The 2014 U.S. Trust Study of High Net Worth Philanthropy.* New York: Author, 2014.

INDEX

The letter a, following a locator, refers to the Appendix.

on philanthropic advisers, 9
on transformational gifts, 104
Friedman, Ann, 24, 72, 82, 103–104
Fullerton, Jessica, 18, 101
Fullerton, John, 18, 83, 101
fundraisers and fundraising
    belief in organization's worth,
        35–37
    communication with and recog-
        nition of philanthropists, 87–88,
        101–102
    confidence in goals, 47–49
    effect of staff and volunteer morale
        on, 68
    identifying and cultivating
        philanthropists/donors, 89–91
    identifying philanthropists'
        objectives, 97–99
    identifying priorities of philan-
        thropists/donors, 93–96
    importance of staff and volunteers
        in, 59–61
    introducing donors to colleagues,
        115–117
    relationship between CEO and
        CDO, 43–45

G

Gates, Bill, 15–16
Gelb, Peter, 23
geography, 97, 120
Gill, Tim, 73, 130
Giving Pledge, 3
givingpledge.org, 3
gratitude, 128–129
guidelines for campaign prediction, 5

H

Harris, Joan, 15–17, 21, 61
health issues, 8, 11, 12
Hebrew University of Jerusalem, 78
Helm, Randy, 46
Hobson, Mellody, 71, 75, 81
Hurst, Robert, 3–4, 82
Hurst, Soledad, 4, 82

I

inclination ratings, 93–96
indebtedness vs. mutual benefit, 127
Indiana University, 36
Inspiring the Largest Gifts of a
    Lifetime, 61
Internet, 90
investments, 8, 25

J

Jewish Theological Seminary, 78

K

Keller, Constance, 71
Keller, Dennis, 18, 82
Kempe, Fred, 76
Korologos, Ann, 72, 82
Kravas, Connie, 87–88
Kroc, Joan, 19

L

Land's End, 54
Lauder, Leonard, 75
lead gifts, 29–31, 36, 40

M

N

O

Obama, Barack, 76
O'Clery, Conor *(The Billionaire Who Wasn't)*, 3

P

Panas, Jerold *(Mega Gifts)*, viii, xix
philanthropic partnership
    appropriate language for, 125–127
    belief of leaders in, 51–56
    board members' practice of, 121–123
    building mutual respect in, 127–128
    families and, 39
    flexibility in, 131–132
    gratitude in, 128–129
    long-term views in, 130
    measuring results in, 129–130
    pride of affiliation and, 139
    qualitative measurements for, 130
    vs. transactional giving, 125
    truth and authenticity in, 130
philanthropic priority, 94–96
philanthropists/donors. *See also* specific individuals
    additional fund-raising and confidence, 29–31
    anonymity, 12, 72
    attributes of, 3
    communication with and recognition of, 101–102
    confidence, lack of, among leadership, 39–41
    financial circumstances, personal, confidence in, 7–9
    historical involvement with organization and, 36
    identifying and cultivating, 4, 89–91
    importance of giving, belief in, 3–6
    introduction of, to one another, 119–120
    involvement with organizations and recipients, 81–83
    leadership, confidence in, 17–20
    leadership, engagement with, 21–25
    mission, belief in, 15–16
    organizational financial planning and stability, confidence in, 25–28
    as partners with organization, 51–56
    partnerships, 75–79
    passion for the mission, 71–73
    personal circumstances, confidence in, 11–14
    philanthropic objectives of, 97–99
    planning process, engagement in, 22
    potential, checklist for, 137a–138a
    practice of philanthropic partnership, 121–123
    priorities of, 93–96
    relationships with colleagues, 87–88, 115–117
    self-solicitation, 25
    time as biggest factor for, 11–14, 81
    vision and confidence in strategy, belief in, 25–28
    volunteer activities of, 103–107
planning, 39–41
Polonsky, Leonard, 5, 77

Polonsky Foundation, 77
President's Commission on the Arts and the Humanities, 77
Pulitzer, Emily, 15
Pulitzer Center on Crisis Reporting, 15

R

Race to the Top, 79
ratings, capacity vs. inclination, 93–96
Ratner, Gerald, 5
Ravinia Women's Board, 83
religion, 5, 12–13
Resnick, Lynda, 72
retirement, 8
Revere School, 54
Rhodes, Frank, viii
Rise Asset Development, 78
risk, 29
Rotman, Joseph, 78, 81
Rotman, Sandra, 21, 26, 78, 97
Rotman School of Management, 78

S

Schiller, Ron (*The Chief Development Officer: Beyond Fundraising*), 46, 64
search committees, 107
shared objective vs. need, 126–127
Sharpe, Robert, 55–56
Siegler, Mark, 77
Simic, Curt, 36
Smith, Rebecca Tseng, 61

staff
    belief and confidence checklist for, 137a–138a
    characteristics of, 65
    confidence in leaders, plans and goals, 63–65
    contribution to fundraising, 48
    development and organization, 61
    importance of, 59–60
    individual contributions, belief in, 67–68
    mission, belief in, 59–61
    relationship building, 115–117
Stanford Graduate School of Education, 61
Strategy, 39–41

T

Tepper, David, 23
term limits, 110–111, 112
Third Way, 106
Thompson, Jim, 136
time
    allocating, along with resources, 71–72
    as factor for donors, 11–14, 81
transformational gifts and giving. *See also* fundraisers and fundraising; philanthropists/donors
    defined, vii
    measurement and proof of impact for, 21
    timing and, 9, 82
Tufts University, 5
turnover, among CDOs, 16

ABOUT THE AUTHOR

Ron Schiller began his development career in the late 1980s at his alma mater, Cornell University, one of the largest and most mature development programs at the time. Prior to joining the development office, as associate director of choral music at Cornell, he raised money for the women's chorus and men's glee club to take concert tours. After he played a lead role in raising $250,000 for a concert tour of Asia, the development office took notice and invited him to join the staff.

In the university development office, Ron served first as assistant director, then as associate director, then as acting director of development for the College of Arts and Sciences, and finally as major gifts officer, focused on gifts of $1 million and above. During those years, as the university undertook higher education's first-ever campaign over $1 billion, Cornell's development staff grew from fewer than 100 to over 300. Ron was fortunate to work with and learn from some of the most highly regarded development professionals in higher education, including and especially Jean Gortzig, Dick Ramin, Inge Reichenbach, and Dave Dunlop.

In 1994, Ron assumed his first senior management position in fundraising at the University of Rochester's Eastman School of Music, where he grew a small staff of three to 10. When the director of the Eastman School left to become president of New England Conservatory, he recruited Ron to join him at the conservatory as vice president for institutional advancement. From there, Ron's career took him to larger and larger offices, including Northeastern University, Carnegie Mellon University, and the University of Chicago, where as vice president he led a team of over 450 staff members that completed a $2.38 billion campaign, established the university's principal gift program, and helped the university secure its first two nine-figure gifts ($100 million and $300 million).

Ron then served as president of the National Public Radio Foundation, leading the development of a national fundraising strategy focused on donors and their overall connection to public radio, a strategy that required a significant increase in the collaboration between NPR and its several-hundred independent member stations. In the first year of a principal gift program established by Ron and his colleagues, NPR had as many seven-figure-gift donors as it had had in all 40 previous years combined.

Ron has served on many boards and advisory councils, including the Cornell University Council, the Cornell University Trustees' Glee Club Advisory Council, the Harris Theater for Music and Dance Board of Trustees, the board of trustees of the North Carolina School of the Arts, the American Academy in Rome Development Committee, and the boards of directors of the American Friends of Covent Garden, the Buddy Program of Aspen, the Cayuga Chamber Orchestra, the Mendelssohn Choir of Pittsburgh, and the Salt Bay Chamberfest, where he is presently board president.

Ron serves as founding partner of the Aspen Leadership Group and the Philanthropy Career Network. He interacts daily with nonprofit leaders and philanthropists and contributes regularly to journals in the field of philanthropy. He is a regular speaker at conferences, including the Council for Advancement and Support of Education's Winter Institute for Chief Development Officers and CASE's annual Inspiring the Largest Gifts of a Lifetime conference.

ABOUT CASE

The Council for Advancement and Support of Education (CASE) is a professional association serving educational institutions and the advancement professionals who work on their behalf in alumni relations, communications, development, marketing and allied areas.

Founded in 1974, CASE maintains headquarters in Washington, D.C., with offices in London, Singapore, and Mexico City. Its membership includes more than 3,600 colleges and universities, primary and secondary independent and international schools, and nonprofit organizations in nearly 80 countries. CASE serves more than 77,000 advancement professionals on the staffs of its member institutions and has more than 17,000 professional members on its roster.

CASE also offers a variety of advancement products and services, provides standards and an ethical framework for the profession, and works with other organizations to respond to public issues of concern while promoting the importance of education worldwide.